Warren J. Brier

A Soldier of Fortune

.

Warren J. Brier

A Soldier of Fortune

ISBN/EAN: 9783337306922

Printed in Europe, USA, Canada, Australia, Japan

Cover: Foto ©Thomas Meinert / pixelio.de

More available books at **www.hansebooks.com**

A Soldier of Fortune

A MODERN COMEDY-DRAMA

IN

FIVE ACTS.

BY

WARREN J. BRIER.

WITH THE

Stage Business, Cast of Characters, Costumes, Time of Representation, Etc.

CHICAGO:
T. S. DENISON.

CAST OF CHARACTERS.

As performed under the direction of the author, by the Plymouth Hub Club, Plymouth, Wis., July 28, 1880.

COL. FITZNOODLE.	MR. C. H. MAYNARD.
MR. PATRONI.	MR. BEVERLY CROCKETT.
MR. BELMONT.	Mr. A. F. WARDEN.
CYRIL CLIFFORD.	Mr. G. W. ZERLER.
DR. FARGO.	Mr. G. L. GILMAN.
FREDDIE BELMONT.	MASTER GEORGIE MATTOON.
SNOWBALL.	MR. E. A. DOW.
BARNEY.	MR. H. E. COTTLE.
MISS AGNES BELMONT.	MISS LILLIE EASTMAN.
MISS IDA LOVEWELL.	MISS MAY DAVIDSON.
MISS PRUCILLA.	MISS MARY CLARK.

SYNOPSIS.

Act I.—General introduction of the characters. The Colonel recounts his war reminiscences. Patroni, the gentleman from California, plots his future villainy. Ida's terror of his threats. His quarrel with Dr. Fargo.

Act II.—Belmont on the verge of bankruptcy. The great robbery at the Belmont Mansion. The Colonel's grand lottery prize.

Act III.—The villainous attempt to blow up Dr. Fargo's office. Fred's remarkable progress in his studies—especially grammar. Snowball has a tooth drawn suddint.

Act IV.—The proposed duel. Serious wounding of the Colonel by Patroni's treachery. Death of the latter by lightning.

Act V.—The great generosity of the Colonel (the soldier of fortune) discovered and rewarded by Belmont. Reconciliation of Agnes and Dr. Fargo. Happy denouement.

STAGE DIRECTIONS.

R means right of stage, facing the audience; L, left; C, center; R C, right of center; L C, left of center. D F, door in the flat, running across the back of the stage; C D F, center door in the flat; R D F, right door in the flat; L D F, left door in the flat; R D, right door; L D, left door; 1 E, first entrance; 2 E, second entrance; U E, upper entrance; 1, 2 or 3 G, first, second or third groove.

Note.—Lightning may be produced by blowing finely powdered rosin into a candle flame; thunder by rattling a large piece of sheet iron; rain by allowing beans to fall through a long narrow box studded on the bottom with pegs, or with oblique partitions leaving a narrow opening on opposite sides alternately; moonlight may be produced by the strong white light of a burning tableau powder.

COSTUMES.

Col.—Uniform of Colonel in U. S. army, full dress with sword, brown wig, sandy mustache and long, sandy side-whiskers, eye-glasses to clasp over nose. In Act III., Scene 2, must have on a very bald iron-gray wig, securely fastened, and over it his brown wig.

Mr. Patroni.—Black wig of wavy hair, combed back of ears, and reaching down to collar of coat; jet-black mustache—long; much jewelry; make-up rich.

Mr. B.—Business suit. In last scene dress-suit; neat wig and beard—iron-gray; age about fifty.

Cyril.—Stylishly dressed. Soft hat in Act III. Scene 1; wig and beard, if any, light colored.

Doctor.—Business suit. Last scene dress suit; wig and beard, if any, brown.

Fred.—Well dressed boy of ten or twelve; prominent watch chain. In Act I wears an old hat.

Snowball.—Black pants and white vest; very large shoes; high standing collar; gaudy tie; swallow-tailed coat; white hat; huge watch chain; huge watch-case with no works; large glass pin, etc.

Barney.—Laborer's suit, very plain; red wig.

Agnes.—Well and tastily dressed in summer suit; auburn wig. Last Act elegant reception toilet.

Ida.—At first appearance dressed in traveling suit of gray or brown; change to a tasty home toilet. Last Act, elegant dress; wig, if any, dark.

Miss P.—A lady of forty dressed like one of twenty; make-up must not disguise the fact that she is an elderly spinster.

PROPERTIES.

Rattan cane, crochet work, letters, kite made of tissue paper on an oval frame, toy pistol with percussion cap, a puppy, marbles, dish of pudding and spoon, a pair of baby's stockings, pasteboard box, lottery tickets, paper in wrap, newspapers, stiletto, books on shelves, small safe at back, revolvers, dark lantern, large knife, sponge, piece of bedcord, lamps, black masks, wooden box fixed to blow flour into face of person who opens it, riding whip, office chairs, book, bottles, glass, small cord, piece of gum for tooth, forceps, phial, blanket, tin can labeled gun powder, taper, matches, ax, novel, placard labeled in large letters, "to please me squeeze me," grammar, pins, cigar, pack of cards, bottle of hair oil, bottle of mucilage, fish pole with small hook on end, rustic seats, rapidly burning fuse for lightning, case for pistols, slips of paper, mirror, bank check.

A SOLDIER OF FORTUNE.

ACT 1.

SCENE.—*Parlor in Belmont Mansion. Marble top table C, holding books and flowers. Arm chair L of table. Small rocking chair R of table. Two other chairs up. Small stand up with shells. Sofa L. Cane in corner.* AGNES *discovered seated at R of center table with crochet work. Enter* MR. B. L *with an open letter.* AGNES *goes up joyfully to meet him.*

Agnes. I'm so glad you have come, papa! (*kisses him*). It has been lonely enough here to-day! (*Leads him to seat at L of table, then sits R of table.*

Mr. B. Cheer up, cheer up, daughter. Your days of loneliness are numbered. This letter from your uncle Lovewell, in California, conveys the intelligence that he is completely broken up in business, and that he has determined to send your cousin Ida here for a few months.

Agnes. (*With great vivacity.*) Ida? That's splendid. Several months, too? I'm delighted. I have been longing of late to see her. But I'm sorry for uncle Edward. It seems too hard that one who has enjoyed for years the luxuries of life should be reduced in his old age to penury. *You* won't fail, will you, papa, and compel us to abandon Belmont Hill and all its luxuriance?

Mr. B. Of course not, child. How it would sound! Belmont, the millionaire, has failed! Ha! ha! Preposterous. (*Aside.*) This is the opportunity, but I haven't the courage to tell her.

Agnes. When will Ida come, papa?

Mr. B. She may come at any time, Agnes. I forgot to mention that she will be accompanied by a gentleman friend, Mr. Albert Patroni.

Agnes. No sweet without its bitter. No pleasure that does not stir up the dregs of pain. I wish her gentleman friend would stay away.

Mr. B. Why such asperity, child, about a stranger? I conjecture by the letter that the gentleman comes out of respect for her father, rather than out of regard for Ida.

Agnes. I hope you conjecture rightly, for it has long been a secret wish of mine that Ida may meet and marry Cyril.

Mr. B. (*Pointedly, and slightly displeased*). And it has long been a secret wish of mine that Cyril may take for a wife some one he has already met, and that person is yourself. As his guardian before he came of age, and his adviser since, I consider that my wishes are entitled to consideration.

Agnes. Cyril seems more like a brother than a lover. Were we to marry it would be a union of hands, but not a union of hearts.

Mr. B. (*Testily.*) Hearts indeed! Young people now-a-days are much too fond of flaunting this heart nonsense into the faces of their elders.

Agnes. Nonsense or not, nothing but the strongest sense of duty could compel me to marry one for whom I have no love.

Mr. B. Well, I'll not argue the matter now. I presume you will have your own way in spite of me. If it suits you better to marry an impecunious physician than a wealthy gentleman, you will undoubtedly do so, though you may live to regret it. Your cousin Cyril comes of a genteel stock. Dr. Fargo is the scion of a family to fortune and fame unknown.

Agnes. Stock and families are all alike to me.
> "The rank is but the guinea's stamp,
> The man's the gowd for a' that,"

and no one can truthfully say that Dr. Fargo is not a gentleman.

Mr. B. True, Agnes, but for a' that, blood will tell.

Agnes. Blood will tell precious little worth noting. Brains can discount blood, nine times in ten. Those old aristocratic notions of blue blood have grown too attenuated for the nineteenth century, and in America at that.

Mr. B. Where did you get such notions, Agnes? You, whose ancestors have all been bankers or brokers.

Agnes. Bankers or brokers, butchers or bakers, what care I? Blue blood has never excelled the common kind in affording motive power to the vast wheels of the world's activity, and it is but fair to presume it never will.

Enter SNOWBALL, L U E, *singing to Little Buttercup:*

> I'm little butcher's pup,
> Pore little butcher's pup,
> Sweet little butcher's pup-pie,
> Dear little——

Mr. B. (*Interrupting him*) Snowball, you must have forgotten your manners.

Sn. No sah. I neber had nun to fohgit. My little brudder got all de mannahs in our fambly.

Agnes. Haven't you often told me, Snowball, that you never had a brother?

Sn. Sartin, Miss Agnes, but can't nobody git nuffin whar dah's nuffin fer nobody ter git? But land of goodness! (*fumbling in his pockets*) I's done fohgot myself. Miser Belmont, I's brung yer up a tally-grammar, ef I kin eber fine it .(*produces it from the back of his neck, and gives it to Agnes*). Dat tally-grammar am in yore uncle Edard's han' writin'? He's a boss penner.

Agnes. What stupidity! Don't you know the operator writes the message? Takes it down just as it comes to him over the line.

Sn. Has you any referentials to de close-line, Miss?

Agnes. (*Impatiently.*) Your ignorance would try the temper of an angel.

Sn. (*Bowing.*) I see it does dat, Miss Agnes.

Mr. B. (*Having read telegram.*) This telegram is from your cousin. She and Mr. Patroni will arrive on the four o'clock train from the West. (*Agnes surprised and joyful. Mr. B. looks at his watch.*) It lacks but twenty minutes of four now. Snowball, have the carriage at the door in ten minutes, and I'll meet them at the train. I must write a letter before I go. Be sharp now, with the carriage. (*Exit R 1 E.*)

Sn. (*Aside.*) Sartin! sartin! I'll be sharp nuff. If I ain't, my appetite will be, an' dat's de importantest part ob me. (*Fumbles in pockets.*) Land of goodness, Miss Agnes, I's got anudder letter yhar. (*Scratches his head.*) Dar! I's jis struck me dat I put it on de end ob de troff when I fed de pigs, an' I'll bet a billion dollahs yas, a *tousand* ob em, ef necessary, dat de lettah has been peroosed by ebery pig in dat pen. I'm one ob em. (*Runs off L.*)

Agnes. Such carelessness! But it's no use to urge papa to send the fellow away. (*Enter Col. R U E.*) His saving Freddie's life when he was drowning, insures his permanence here (*sees Col. aside.*) Here is our Soldier of Fortune.

Col. (*Down to R and Bowing.*) Instrumental in saving Freddie's life, was he? That's gratifying to a soldier, though performed by a person of race and color, etc.

Agnes. Yes, Colonel, we must admire the heroic, in whomsoever found.

Col. You appear to be something of a hero-worshiper, Miss Belmont.

Agnes. Not exactly that, perhaps. Still, I admire heroic deeds.

Col. Sad, isn't it, how things have changed since the days of that old Greecy poet, can't think of his name, you know.

Agnes. Homer?

Col. Exactly! exactly! Wrote so much about wars, and heroes, and gods. Beautiful descriptions of grand armies, with their streaming, brilliant banners, and their glistening muskets and——

Agnes. You don't mean muskets, Colonel. They didn't fight with muskets in those days.

Col. No, of course they didn't. That was merely a *vice verse,* a slip of the tongue, you know. I recollect now they fought with sticks, at least in all their accounts of battles they speak frequently of crossing the Sticks.

Agnes. You don't understand, Colonel. The Styx was the name of a river, and not the name of weapons of warfare.

Col. Oh, ah, indeed.

Agnes. Yes. But where have you been all day, Colonel? It has been lonely here, with papa and Cyril in the city, Fred in the woods robbing birds' nests, and Miss Peterson busy on her tract on "Cruelty to Animals."

Col. I, too, have been engaged in literary labor. Establishing a formula for the striking force of any aggregated portion of material. Perhaps you don't grasp my meaning.

Agnes. Yes, I think I do. (*Scream without.*)

Fred. (*Outside, very loudly.*) Give that back! Give it back, I say, or I'll smash you, you ebony-colored idiot! I found it, and I'll have it. (*Scuffling without. Col. acts timid and draws his sword.*)

Enter Sn. L I E, *with a letter—large.*

Sn. Here am de lettah, Miss Agnes (*gives it*). Fred was slidin' down de banister onto it (*Agnes reads it. Aside.*) Dem pigs didn't eben open de letter, to say nuffin' ob readin' it. Dey looks down on de 'Merican language jis case dey war wunst owned by a Frenchman. Dey's too Frenchy fer nuffin'. I'm one ob 'em. (*Col. has taken some tickets from his pocket and slyly looked them over.*)

Col. (*Aside.*) To-day is the long-expected time. To-day wealth and independence may be mine. Then good-by to hook and crook, to sham and show. The Georgetown lottery draws to-day, and with five good tickets I may suddenly find myself rolling in confluence. (*Puts tickets carefully away.*)

Agnes. (*Having finished the letter.*) This letter is of no consequence, Snowball, but another time don't be so careless.

Sn. Yaas; I guess I won't. I war dreffully afeared dat it war one ob de Doctah's conscriptions fer de heart diseases. I'm one ob 'em.

Agnes. (*Sternly.*) Leave the room at once, sir. (*Exit Sn. hastily to L.*) Talk of patient Job. He should have had that fellow for his servant.

Col. He'd have been boiling most of the time, I imagine. Being patient reminds me of a circumstance, I think it was just before the battle of Bean Ridge. Yours truly was captured while playing a quiet little game of " I spy," and was sentenced to be shot at noon. The patience I exhibited in waiting for my midday repast was something beautiful to see. It would have made that boiler you just now mentioned go and conceal his cranial antimony. (*Enter* Miss Peterson *R U E.*) Perhaps you don't grasp my meaning, but war is a cruel, cruel employment, Miss Belmont.

Miss P. (*Coming down.*) How very unpleasant it must be to engage in military occupations. And were you really in the nasty war, dear Colonel Fitznoodle?

Col. (Pompously.) Certainly, certainly. Fought all through the war. Was in every battle of it.

Agnes. I suppose you did some of the hardest fighting at the battle of Gettysburg?

Col. (Thoughtfully.) Gettysburg? Yes, yes. We had tough beef and hard-tack for breakfast that day, and they gave me such an attack of dyspepsia that the attack of the enemy was no pleasure to me. I did not enjoy that battle, not in the least. I always like chicken salad or fried oysters for breakfast when there is any prospect of an engagement.

Miss P. (Archly.) Agnes, didn't we have chicken salad for breakfast this morning?

Agnes. I think we did.

Miss P. (Nods suggestively to Col. Aside.) Then perhaps there is a prospect of an engagement to-day, if he can take such a gentle hint as that. *(To Col.)* But isn't there a great deal of danger in a battle?

Col. (Thoughtfully.) Oh—well—yes, considerable. No uncommon thing for some of the parties to get badly injured. *I* have known of some frightful accidents in battle.

Miss P. (With emotion.) Dreadful, dreadful. Why do people frequent such places? Why doesn't our Legislature pass a law compelling people to stay away from battles?

Agnes. You should have your society get up a petition to that effect, and send it in with your labor petition.

Col. I—I—I hope you are not getting up a petition that will cause the Legislature to pass any statuary compelling people to labor.

Miss P. No, no. We are petitioning the Legislature to pass a law to prevent organ-grinders from making the monkeys labor more than six hours a day. Poor little unfortunate things *(wipes her eyes.*

Col. Oh, ah, yes, I see, I see. A monkey law. *(Aside.)* Well, that doesn't apply to me. *(Direct.)* Even laws relating to taxes concern me but little. But the subject of labor to me is a matter of muscular importance.

Agnes. (Laughing.) Ah, Colonel, I fear this conversation is a matter of too great muscular importance, so I'll withdraw. Be so kind as to come and assist me for a few moments, Miss Peterson. The Colonel will perhaps be glad to excuse us so he can have a little rest from the fatigue of conversation.

Col. Oh, no, no, no, no. *(Exit AGNES and MISS P. R U E.* *Col. takes out tickets and examines them, looking at ladies' place of exit.)* Adorable *(looks at tickets)* pasteboards. In you lies the power to confer wealth and all the pleasing pandemonium that word implies. This hour I am destitute. Possessed of naught save my trusty blade and the neuralgia *(putting hands to side of his head.)* Not a dollar to my name, except this confounded ticdoloureux *(he should pronounce it tic-dollar-oo.)* Next hour I am rolling in luxury--perhaps. The favored child of fortune. With wealth at

mv command I might woo and win the adorable Miss Peterson.
While poverty is my lot I'll not chance the matrimonial lottery.

Enter Sᴺ. *L carrying a box.*

Sn. Yhar's some express office, sah, an' yhar's some post office,
sah (*puts box on chair, gives paper. Exit L.*)
Col. (*Tears open paper wrap and reads.*) The following is a list
of the numbers taking prizes in the Georgetown lottery, the drawing of which took place to-day. *Bus. of comparing his number with
list.*) Here it is! Here it is! No. 3843. Hurrah for 3843! Glorious!
Sublime! Sublimary! Translucent. (*Sees box, reads from cover.*)
" From Georgetown Lottery. Prize corresponding to No. 3843."
Perhaps it's the grand prize, a gold brick worth $50,000. My luck
must change some time (*opening box and unrolling a large bundle of
paper, wrap after wrap*), and now is the time. My evil genius
certainly will not blast my tender quickening hopes (*discovers a
pair of baby's stockings.*) Oh! Blast my tender quickening hopes.
What a fool ! (*holding them up to view.*) What an idiot. Five tickets
at five dollars each. Five certificates to convince an unforgiving
world that I'm an ass. Twenty-five dollars gone for a pair of
stockings too small for the legs of the wild *chemise* that bounds the
Alps among.

Enter Miss P. *R U E.* Col. *hastily puts stockings in pocket;
throws papers in box, and box under chair.*

Miss P. Dear, dear, what a giddy young thing Agnes is! But
we girls are pretty much alike, after all.
Col. (*Bowing confusedly.*) Indeed we are, Miss Peterson.   Indeed we are.
Miss P. I'm almost dying, Colonel, to hear some of your interesting war reminiscences. Tell me

> " Of most disastrous chances
> Of moving accidents by flood and field ;
> Of hairbreadth scapes, "

and I will shed copious tears, as did Desdemona at the recountal
of Othello's dangers.
Col. I cannot resist appeal so eloquent. I'll tell you of an accident which happened to the husband's brother of my aunt's wife.
(*They sit partly facing audience.*) This fellow was a novice at war,
and when the battle began he seized a link of stovepipe from a coal
stove the boys were erecting——
Miss P. (*Hitching her chair closer and closer to Col.'s.*) A coal
stove in the army?
Col. Certainly. Couldn't keep warm without, you know. Well,
this gentleman, while hurrying along, stepped upon a—a—why
can't I think of the name of that thing the soldiers wear on the
ends of their guns—now I have it—bayonet—stepped upon a bayonet that some careless fellow had left right in the path, and ran the

wretched thing clear through his pedal extremity. Perhaps you
don't grasp my meaning. (*Wipes his face with baby's socks.*) An
ambuscade drove up just then and conveyed the poor fellow to the
hospital. (*Drops one of the socks on floor and puts other in pocket.*)

Miss P. (*Wiping her eyes.*) Oh, horrible, and we living in a
land prolific of Legislatures, too. (*Puts her head gently on* Col.'s
shoulder. Col. *looks nervous.*

Enter Fred L U E. *In R hand a hooped kite, in other a toy percussion pistol.*

Fred. (*Aside.*) A couple of spoons. I'll put them into hot
water. (*Slips down behind them, yells, slaps kite over* Col.'s *head,
leaving hoop around his neck.* Col. *and* Miss P. *spring to their feet,*
Fred *fires the pistol at them, gives two or three terrific yells, and
runs off R 1 E.* Miss P. *partly faints into* Col.'s *arms.* Col. *helps
her to a seat on sofa, then draws his sword.* Cyril *and* Agnes *hurry
in from R U E.*

Cyril. What seems to be the trouble here?

Col. (*Amazed and trembling*). I—I—I thought we were having
an earthquake.

Agnes. (*Amused, aside*). He a Colonel! I don't believe he
ever *saw* a regiment of soldiers, let alone commanded one. (*To*
Col. *pointing to kite frame around his neck*). Is this a new style in
neckties, Colonel?

Col. (*Astonished.*) How did that get there? Help me take it
off, quick. People might take me for an acrobat practicing for a
circus.

Enter Mr. B., Mr. Patroni *and* Ida D *in* F. Col. *rushes off
R with hoop still on.* Ida *and* Agnes *rush into each other's arms.
Bus. of introducing* Mr. P. *and* Ida *to* Cyril *and* Miss P., *and*
Mr. P. *to* Agnes.

Mr. B. Daughter, you may conduct your cousin to the blue
room, and you, Cyril, may lead the way for Mr. Patroni to the
north chamber. They need an opportunity to make themselves
more comfortable after their long journey. (*To* Mr. P.) Your
trunks have preceded you. I hope, sir, you will experience no dis-
comfort while you remain with us.

Mr. P. Don't fear for me. I have the faculty of adapting myself to all sorts of surroundings. (*Exit R.* Cyril *and* P, Agnes *and*
Ida.

Mr. B. (*Aside*). All sorts of surroundings, indeed. He is evidently just what he claims to be, a gentleman. (*Enter* Col. R.
*with kite removed, and toe of stocking protruding from breast of his
coat*). How have *you* fared to-day, Colonel? Haven't been
afflicted with *ennui*, I hope?

Col. Oh, no, indeed! Not at all! I hardly think Ong Wee has been here. Chinaman, I suppose? Don't think I noticed him if he was here. I'm so absent minded.   At the battle of Brandy and Wine, when Meade ordered Porter to attack the enemy's retrenchments, I came near annihilating my own brother.   He called out Alphonso Adolphus Fitznoodle, what are you thinking about, and thereby saved his life. (*Enter* Sn. *D in F.*)

Miss P. That came near being another Cain and Abel tragedy.

Sn. (*Excitedly*). Has Caman Abel got de traggaydies, Miss?

Miss P. I referred to Cain, who killed his brother, Abel.

Sn. Did he, Miss? Dat's meaner dan de chap you read to me 'bout in de good book what et de cheese and den gub de pore widder de mite.   Next time I see dat walkin' stick I'll put a head on him, sartin shore.   Hangin's too good fer him.   He orter hef ter hoe taters all day in de hot sun.

Mr. B. You seem to think hanging trifling compared with hoeing.   So leave your work for to-day and take yourself off fishing. (*Exit* Mr. B. *R.*)

Sn. No use fer me ter go fishin', case I's been swarin'. Ef yer swars yer can't ketch no fish.

Miss P. (*Consolingly, and anxious to get rid of him*). Oh, I guess you didn't say anything very bad, Snowball.

Sn. Yes I did.   I called Fred a blear-eyed cypher.

Col. (*Patronizingly*). Can't you go and look for Freddie? That's a good boy.

Sn. (*Positively*). Wouldn't like to do it, sah, if he *is* a good boy.   I's afeard I shud find him, an' I doesn't need him no more dan a cat needs a compass.

Col. (*Disgusted, aside*). No use to bandage words with that coal-colored infidel.   I believe he persists in staying just to be annoying. (*Direct*). Won't you have the unmitigated kindness to transport that receptacle to my somniferous apartment?

Sn. Which? (*In stupid wonder*).

Col. Take that box to my bedroom, as it were. You don't seem to grasp my meaning.   (Sn. *exits R with box.*   Miss P. *discovers stocking on floor and picks it up gingerly, between thumb and finger*).

Miss P. How came this article of apparel here, I wonder? (*Looks inquiringly at* Col. *and sees other stocking in breast of his coat.   Snatches it and holds it up before him.   Fiercely*). What means this, sir?   By what strange freak does it devolve upon you to be the possessor of a pair of these?   Have you not told me that you are unmarried?   That you never have been married?

Col. I—I—upon my soul it is the merest accident; I didn't mean to, indeed I didn't.

Miss P. Accident!   Didn't mean to get married, I suppose.

Col. No, no, no.   Didn't mean that you should find it out.

Miss P. That's consoling.

Col. I mean—I mean that I didn't intend to have any one see them (*Enter* Sn). It's all a mistake, an accident, I tell you

They were sent to me without my knowledge or consent. I don't want them. I haven't any more use for them than—you have.

Sn. (*Aside, holding up foot*). Guess dey'd fit me.

Miss P. I fear you are trying to better one falsehood by another.

Sn. I'll swar to its troof, Miss. I brung in de box, an' after I got out de key hole happened to git close to my eye an' I seed him take 'em out ob dat box. Dat's his gran' prize from de lottery. Yah, yah. I'm one ob 'em.

Miss P. (*Mollified*). I beg pardon, Colonel, for my display of temper. So you are not a married man, after all? (*Laughs hysterically*).

Col. Not in the least. I'm very much unmarried. Here, Snowball, you may become the single owner of this double prize.

Sn. Tanks, sah. Dey'll be good to hold ten cent pieces—ef I eber gits any.

Col. I have some in my room. I'll get you a brace of them. (*Exit R*).

Enter Fred, leading a pup.

Fred. (*Loudly and rapidly*). Snowball, run for the doctor, and tell him to bring two pounds of dog's-bane. This cur has just swallowed my new slate, sponge and all. He can keep the slate, but I'm bound to make him throw up the sponge. (*Sn. kicks pup in ribs.* Miss P. *takes him by ear and leads him down*).

Sn. Ou—ch! Jew-peter and Slattern! O—h! Wish 't I war an alligator, den I wouldn't git sech treatment from a member ob de society for prevention cruelty to alligators.

Miss P. (*Letting go*). Stupid! Our society is for preventing cruelty to animals.

Sn. Ain't alligators animals? 'Sides I warn't doin' no harm. Jes testin' dat dog's tenacity by seein' ef de slate ud jingle.

Miss P. (*Cuffing him*). That's to see if the brass in your face will jingle.

Sn. (*Aside*). Durn sight more *tingle* dan *jingle*.

Miss P. Another time perhaps you will not linger in the parlor and interrupt the conversation of the ladies and gentlemen. (*Exit R, loftily*).

Fred. (*Who has had biz up, training dog*). Serves you right, smudge, for interfering with the sweet things and their loveyers. If you had gone after the doctor, you would have saved yourself a blistered jaw.

Sn. Ef you doan shut up I shan't show you dem strawberries wot I foun' dis mornin'.

Fred. (*In a wheedling tone*). Never mind, Snowball, I didn't mean no harm, honor bright, hope to die if I did. She's a mean old thing, *ain't* she. Swats a feller fearful careless, don't she? If you'll show me the strawberries, I'll give you a glassy and three brownies (*gives marbles*.) and I'll let you chew my gum all the forenoon to-morrow. (*Aside*). That's liberal, seein' the gov'nor told me he'd warm me if I don't quit chewing it myself.

Sn. I'll do it, Fred, if you'll hook me a dish of puddin' from de kitchen table. Wouldn't ax yer to do it but I's got de gout in my shoulder and can't walk very well. (*Exit* FRED *R with pup*). Ya, ya, dat's a bad ailin', but I reckon a littie puddin' will cure it Guess I'll sing myself to sleep.

(*Sings to Silver Threads Among the Gold*).

> Darling I am growing old,
> Silber treads among de gold,
> If you'd keep me young and fair
> Buy for me some bettah hair.
> But my darling you must know, you know
> Dat de times am fearful slow,
> An' dat switch you tink so ill,
> Cost a nineteen dollar bill.
> Yes you know I'm growin'—

Enter MR. B. *R. U E.*

Mr. B. (*Interrupting song*). Calling for your dinnei, are you Snowball?

Sn. Yes, sah. (*Aside*). He'll say so when dat young hyena comes up wif de puddin'. (*Exit* SN. *L*).

Mr. B. My plans are shattered now. I could see it in the first glance of Cyril's eye. She made a strong first impression. Alas! what shall I do next? Little did Agnes think to-day when she spoke of my failing, how very near I am to the verge of financial ruin. Think of it. The millionaire, possessor of only a few paltry thousands in bonds, and the roof over his head. Under obligation to his ward's fortune for a large share of that, too. Had I not meddled with Cyril's fortune, I might at least have been saved from dishonor. The fear that he will demand a settlement is a daily torture. If Aggie's marriage with him could be brought about, all would be well. I'm not yet so base as to tell her my misfortunes to induce her to consent to the marriage. I'll die first.

(*Enter* CYRIL *and* MR. P.)

Mr. B. (*Starts, confused*). Did you have a pleasant journey, Mr. Patroni?

Mr. P. (*Disgusted*). Journey? Humph! The most infernal bore a gentleman knows. One is surrounded by such coarse people even in the palace coaches! They ought to be compelled to walk, with their disgusting children screaming for bottles; their repulsive conversation, and their impertinent questions. Bah! The whole thing sickens me to think of it.

Cyril. (*Aside*). On the whole he seems to be rather a sickish fellow.

Enter FRED *hastily R, stops when in front of* MR. P., *holding dish of pudding in front of him.*

Fred. (*Without looking up*). Here it is at last, glutton. (*Sees gents*). Hallo! (*Sits up and eats*).

Mr. B. (*Sharply*). Fred, how often must I tell you not to wear your hat in the house?

Fred. Who cares for the wear and tear of an old hat like this? I traded two kittens for it. Miss Peterson told me to drown. I guess I can afford to wear it, if it *is* in the house.

Mr. B. Betake yourself to your room, boy, or I shall be obliged to punish you.

Fred. Steady now, boss; I am not a drum, so you'd better not beat me. (MR. B. *takes cane from corner and strikes him over the shoulders.* FRED *roars out. Enter* SN. *L*).

Mr. B. Here, Snowball, take this impertinent boy to his room, and keep him there until he is willing to act civilly. (SN. *has bus. in getting* FRED *off, struggling.*)

Mr. P. (*Aside*). That boy is a stunner; got the mouth of a shark and the voice of a calliope.

Mr. B. Suppose we take a stroll on the lawn, Mr. Patroni, where we can enjoy a smoke in quiet. (MR. P. *bows assent*). Will you accompany us, Cyril?

Cyril. Thanks, but I believe it's more comfortable here. (*Exit* MR. B. *and* MR. P. *D M F.* Cyril *throws himself on a sofa*). That is certainly one of the most incorrigible boys in the universe. Hell! (*Looking up sees* AGNES *and* IDA *who have entered R, and continues rising*), was known to the ancient Greeks as Hades.

Agnes. You are profanely negligent about connecting the parts of your sentences, Cyril.

Cyril. I hope not. You see our angelic Freddie made me think of Greek fire,—it's such a job to put him out. Greek fire very naturally made me think of Hades.

Ida. (*To* AGNES). Is your brother such a nice little fellow?

Agnes. I'll not answer that. Wait until you form his acquaintance.

Cyril. He's a pink of perfection. None know him but to love him. The fact is, uncle has been too much employed "on Change" to give much supervision to such an inconsequential thing as a boy, and that accounts for it.

Ida. The poor little fellow should be pitied, not blamed.

Agnes. After all, there are some good things about Freddie.

Cyril. Yes, that's true; but it is a trifle saddening to think they are chiefly furnished him by the tailor.

Agnes. (*Going.*) You are too severe on Fred, but I cannot stay longer to take his part.

Cyril. Never fear for him. He'll take his own part, and much more too, I'll warrant.

Agnes. Now, Cyril, try to make yourself agreeable to Ida in my absence. You know her happiness here depends largely upon you.

Cyril. No more agreeable task can be assigned me. (*Exit* Ag-nes *R*). I shall be most happy in endeavoring to make your stay here pleasant.

Ida. Thank you. I have no doubt but that, so far as circum-stances will permit, you will succeed in your efforts.

Cyril. (*To L, aside*). "So far as circumstances will permit;" I don't understand that. (*Enter* Sn. *R*). She's perfectly charming, any way.

Sn. (*To* Cyril). 'Scuse me, but Mr. Belmont wants to see you in de souf chamber imejit. (*Aside, with a glance at* Cyril *and* Ida). Dar is people in dis wuld what's dead in love. (*Starts off R, stops, and looks back*). I'm one ob em. (*Exit R.* Mr. P. *stands in D in F*).

Cyril. I must leave you, Miss—Ida. Excuse the liberty I take in calling you so. To-morrow I will show you some of our charm-ing scenery.

Ida. Thank you. I long to see the beautiful Hudson, and com-pare its scenery with the grandeur of my own State.

Cyril. You can scarcely hope to find it impressive. When in distant lands our fond imaginations give to scenes of home pris-matic coloring, while our eyes behold surrounding scenes dressed in the plain garb of reality. But I must not stay longer (*Seizes her hand and kisses it warmly*). Farewell, we'll meet in the morning. (*Exit L, 1 E without seeing* Mr. P. *up*).

Ida. Ah, yes! (*Sighs.*) Will meet in the morning. (*Senti-mental song may here be introduced.* Mr. P. *comes down at close of song*).

Mr. P. (*Sneeringly*). What nonesense is this, madam? Are we already sentimental over this young dandy? Upon my soul, we are getting on astonishingly.

Enter Col. *R U E, unseen by* Patroni. *Motions off R, and* Sn. *enters.* They come down R. Mr. P. *and* Ida L.

Ida. (*Grieved*). You have no reason to address me thus (*with spirit*) and I'll not submit to it.

Mr. P. You'll not submit to it? Ha, ha! By heavens, that's rich! Madam, you seem to forget who you are. (*They are par-tially facing audience*).

Col. (*Aside to* Sn). I'll paralyze him with a glance of my eye, and you may pulverize him with— (*Pummels him in dumb show*).

Mr. P. Now let me tell you that *I'll* not submit to any more of this sentimentalism with that young popinjay, and you may as well know it first as last. (Sn. *scowls, and in dumb show knocks him down and drags him out*). Decide at once. Ten minutes is all the time required to send to San Francisco a message that would cause your dear, pious, hypocritical old father's immediate arrest. It would furnish him with a cell in the penitentiary, for *he is a felon*. (Ida *sinks upon sofa.* Sn. *seizes* Mr. P. *by his coat collar, spins him around, and gives him a blow that sends him tumbling into R U corner; seizes a large, jagged shell from table, and leans over* Mr. P).

Sn. (*Threatening him with the shell*). Lie still, honey, or I'll shell you, sartin shure. I'm one ob 'em.

(COL. *has advanced to sofa, and is bowing suavely to* IDA.)

Col. The united efforts of the paralyzer and the pulverizer have compelled him to pause. The California cad cowers in yonder corner, sic semper fisticuff.

CURTAIN.

ACT II.

SCENE I. *Same as Scene in Act I. Screen up at back near R U E. A man standing behind the screen, partly visible to audience, but not recognizable by them.*

Enter MR. B. *and* CYRIL *R* 1 *E.*

Mr. B. So you demand an immediate settlement of your estate, I am to understand.

Cyril. Not demand, uncle. Demand would sound highly presumptuous.

Mr. B. The fact is, business is pressing just now, and a complete settlement would greatly inconvenience me. Would a few days make any great difference?

Cyril. Certainly not, uncle, only I am getting tired of this aimless life. I design to marry before long, and settle down to business for myself.

Mr. B. I trust you have not made your choice of a wife without consulting me. Your father, before he died, requested that I should advise with you in that matter.

Cyril. Choice? Not yet. But, guardy, couldn't you advance me something in a day or two? There's a beautiful property in the city, I can buy at a bargain. Its value will double, shortly.

Mr. B. How much would be required for that?

Cyril. One hundred thousand dollars.

Mr. B. (*Alarmed, aside*). More than the sum total of all my ready funds. (*Direct.*) All right. Come down to the office to-morrow, and we'll see about it. I have partly enough in the safe in the library, but it has a time lock, and will not open until four in the morning. I hope that will quiet your distrust, sir.

Cyril. Distrust? I have none. Of course, such a thing as a guardian appropriating the funds in his care is not an unheard of event, but I hope you do not think I suspect you of anything wrong.

Mr. B. Of course you don't. Never mind about it, but come round to-morrow.

Cyril. (*Aside*). His talk of suspicion has aroused suspicion. Guess I'd better be on my guard. Familiarity with bulls and bears has torn the cloak of honor from many a man. (*Exit.*)

Mr. B. (*In a lower tone.*) One hundred thousand dollars, and only fifty thousand dollars to meet the demand. Aggie's diamond necklace must go first and unless my fortune changes, this beautiful home will soon follow it. I'll get them from the safe at daylight and take them to the city. It seems almost like theft, but there is no help for it. (*Exit R. Man behind screen moves off unrecognized.*)

Enter COL. L.

Col. Good morning. (*Looks about surprised.*) Nobody here? Was certain I heard voices. (MR. P. *saunters in R smoking, throws himself into a chair, pays no heed to* COL.) Good morning, Mr. Patroni. How do you find yourself this morning?

Mr. P. In the same way I *usually* find myself when I *lose* myself; wait for some fool to bring me to myself.

Col. I mean what is the condition of your constitutional organism?

Mr. P. Haven't one in my possession, sir. Now by the way Corporal—

Col. (*Correcting him*). Colonel, sir, colonel.

Mr. P. All the same so far as you are concerned. You have, seen fit to quiz me, let me ask you a question. Why do you resemble this stiletto? (*Shows one.*)

Col. (*Thoughtfully.*) We both possess a trusty blade. (*Touches sword.* MR. P. *shakes his head.*) We're both keen, cutting, you know.

Mr. P. I asked for points of resemblance, not for dissimilarities.

Col. Now I have it. We both have a good deal of steel in us. (*Hastily corrects himself.*) No, no no, I don't mean that. We're both fierce and bloodthirsty, and both wear shoulder-straps, at least I do. That's what I mean.

Mr. P. No, sir. You resemble this stiletto because neither of you can take a hint and shut up.

Col. (*Angry, going up.*) Indeed, sir, indeed. My resemblance to your palmetto is only equaled by your resemblance to a pitchy porcupine. Perhaps you don't grasp my meaning? (*Exit* COL. *haughtily to L.*)

Mr. P. The stupid! If I were master here, that valiant military genius would take his uniform and rattling sword off the premises in double quick. Belmont tolerates him because the fellow nursed him during a fever, just as he tolerates that doctor, I suppose, because *he* nurses *other* people during fevers. (*Enter* AGNES *R U E.*) I hate the shilly-shally coward. I verily believe he fears his own shadow.

Agnes. (*Coming down.*) Perhaps he is not such a coward as you imagine, Mr. Patroni.

Mr. P. (*Rising, and taking her hand warmly.*) I beg your pardon, Miss Belmont, if I have offended.

Agnes. No apology is necessary, Mr. Patroni. I only hope you do not misjudge the Colonel. Beneath a vain and frivolous exterior ofttimes beats a heart as true as steel, a soul more noble than that of belted knight or lofty-titled squire.

Mr. P. That sounds well, Miss Belmont, but I fear this valiant Soldier of Fortune, as he loves to call himself, could be chased with a dagger of lath.

Agnes. As to that, I cannot say; but silly and vain as he is, I am inclined to think there is some latent courage in his make-up that only time and circumstance can reveal. But this is too prosy for a balmy morning in June. (*Enter* CYRIL. *R. Introduce song by* AGNES, *if convenient.*) Come, I want to show you some of my varieties of tulips. (*They go up.*) Won't you go with us, Cyril?

Cyril. No, thank you. No new tulips for me. The common kind suits me admirably.

Agnes. (*Coming back.*) So I have often observed.

> The tulips for you
> Are the lips of two.

(CYRIL *seizes her and gives her a loud kiss; she follows* MR. P. *off at back, shaking her finger threateningly at* CYRIL.)

Cyril. *Looking out of window.*) I fear she cares something for that Mexican after all. But why need I care? If he only proves genuine, what is it to me? And yet, (*enter* IDA, *R 1 E, coughs, but does not attract his attention,*) as there seem no hope in the other direction, I have half a mind to propose to Agnes myself. I might win her in spite of learned doctor, or lofty dodger, either one. 'Twould please uncle immensely. (*Turnes and sees* IDA, *stops confused.*)

Ida. (*Agitated.*) Forgive me, Mr. —, Cyril, I mean. I unintentionally overheard you; I tried to attract your attention, but—

Cyril. There is no harm done.

Ida. You do love cousin Agnes then, don't you? I'm so glad. She's a dear, good girl, and you couldn't help being happy with her. (*Goes to window to hide her emotion.*)

Cyril. (*Down, aside.*) This is highly interesting, I declare. Each is very anxious to marry me—to the other. Agnes hopes I'll marry Ida, "she's so sweet," (*imitating*) and Ida hopes I'll marry Agnes, "she's such a dear, good girl" (*imitating.*) They're a precious pair to each other. It isn't so nice to be a shuttle knocked back and forth to form the web and woof of life. This thing has got to stop.

Ida. (*Coming down.*) I hope you have decided to try to win her; she'll make you a charming wife, Cyril.

Cyril. I have decided.

Ida. (*Sinking into a chair*). I'm so glad.

Cyril. (*Aside.*) She looks almost beside herself with joy. Her tongue says one thing, and her face another. (*Rests arm on her chair.*) Can you encourage me in taking such a step, Miss Love-well?

Ida. (*With an effort at cheerfulness.*) Oh yes, indeed.

Cyril. (*To L, aside.*) Confound it! Does she love the Mexican, and hope that I will get Agnes out of her way? (*Sits by her side.*) Ida, you cannot be entirely unconscious of the all absorbing love for you that has filled my heart ever since you came here.

Ida. Please don't, Mr. Clifford. I must not hear another word. Leave me at once, I beg of you. (*Looks around in terror.*)

Cyril. But will you send me away without one word of encouragement?

Ida. (*Hastily.*) Yes, yes. I have no word of encouragement to give. (CYRIL *rises stiffly, she detains him.*) Please do not leave me in anger, I did not wish to offend you.

Cyril. You *do* love me then? You will be mine?

Ida. I cannot be yours. The obstacles are insurmountable. Marry you I cannot; give you a reason, I dare not. Honor must remain inviolate, though the brain goes wild and the heart break. (*Breaks down and hurries off, sobbing.*)

Cyril. (*Sinking into a chair, and hiding face in hands*). Lost forever! (*Enter* MISS P. D *in F, comes down and sees* CYRIL.)

Miss P. Indigestion? (*No answer*). Touch of colic, perhaps. It's all right, though. The doctor just now rode into the yard. Quite providential.

Cyril. Curse the doctor.

Miss P. Mercy! What for? The doctor never injured me; besides, I never swear. (*Enter* DOCTOR D *in F.*) Your coming is fortunate, Doctor. This young gentleman seems to be ailing.

Dr. (*Pleasantly.*) Good morning, Mr. Clifford. Are you indisposed, this morning?

Cyril. (*Savagely.*) No, sir. Quite the contrary. I am very much *disposed* to mind my own business.

Dr. You should surely be accorded that privilege, especially as so few of us feel that way inclined.

Cyril. Your sarcasm, sir, is no more acceptable than it is uncalled for.

Dr. I beg your pardon; I intended neither sarcasm nor offense.

Miss P. I know he's ailing, doctor, or he would not display such temper. Don't you think he needs a dose of pennyroyal tea?

Cyril. (*Springing up.*) Pennyroyal, nonesense! When I want your valuable suggestions, I'll inform you. Until then, I'll bid you good day. (*Exit D in F.*)

Dr. Guess we've caught a Tartar; he'd better confine himself to a diet of lemons, it might sweeten him.

Miss P. I'll keep watch of him. I think there must be something wrong with his mind; he seems to be out of his head.

Dr. If he is out of his head, he has evidently got out through the mouth. (*Exit D in F.*)

CHANGE.

SCENE II. *Library in Belmont Mansion. Safe at back. Light down, but not too dark. Two or three easy chairs. Books on shelves.*

Enter PATRONI *and an assistant disguised in old clothing and black cloth over faces. They carry revolvers, a dark lantern and a huge knife.*

Mr. P. (*In a disguised voice.*) This is the room, and this the safe. Now for business. Fifty thousand dollars and a diamond necklace. (*Kneels before safe and tries the combination.*) No use. There is only one way; we must request the gentleman, who knows the combination, to come and open it. (*Exit L. COL. sticks his head, encased in a night cap, in from D at R.*)

Col. Am I waking, or am I dreaming? (*Enters but partly dressed.*) It's more than probable I do. It struck me that I heard sound in here that resembled the human voice, struck me so forcibly that it knocked me out of bed. It's hardly safe to be here in this undressed uniform. (*Listens.*) I must have been deceived. The tic douloureux isn't at par as a burglar alarm. It'ssafe to say the safe is safe; so while I'm safe I'll—(*stops and begins to tremble, goes to L and looks off.*) Discretionary, thou art a jewel! *Takes two or three long, swift strides off R.*)

Enter L the two burglars with MR. B. *between them, he is half-dressed, gagged and blindfolded.*

Mr. P. (*In same disguised voice.*) Now, make haste. It's after four o'clock and day will soon break. Go at that combination, old man, and no cursed nonsense. (MR. B. *does not move.*) You hear this? (*Tapping the large knife on the safe.*) If that safe isn't open in sixty seconds, your hand will never open it. (*Counts off the seconds from his watch, by the light of the lantern.*) Five, ten, fifteen, twenty, twenty-five, thirty. Thirty more, and you die. Thirty-five, forty. (MR. B. *stoops, grasps the knob, gives it a few turns and as the word sixty is spoken swings safe door open.* PATRONI *pulls out money drawer. Enter* COL. D *in R cautiously, with sword in one hand and sponge dipped in ink in the other. Spatters the men with the ink, then skips off R. Burglar sees him and is about to fire.* MR. P. *stops him.*)

Mr. P. Now the cord, quick, or the fool will alarm the house. (*Hastily bind* MR. B. *to safe, and run off to* L. *Enter* COL. *cautiously; dressed, and carrying a lighted lamp. Hastily liberates* MR. B.)

Mr. B. Ruined, completely ruined. The rascals have taken money, diamonds, everything.

Col. Oh, no, not everything. They left us our lives and our safe and our sword and our tic douloureux.

Mr. B. Didn't you hear them until they fled?

Col. Certainly, certainly. Heard them and spotted them.

Mr. B. But why didn't you bring your sword to my assistance, and save the valuables?

Col. I— I— oh, I had a valuable of my own to save. *I* value my *life.* For strange as it may seem, when this is gone I can't pick up another. I saw they did not mean to hurt you, so I decided not to hurt them. Besides, there were two of them and one of me. Had there been one of them and two of me I should have looked upon it differently. I never forget that consistency is the better part of valor. But come, we stand here splitting hairs when we were better employed in splitting heads. (*Exit both to R.*)

CHANGE.

SCENE III. *Scene same as Act I.*

Enter AGNES *followed by* MR. P.

Agnes. (*Speaking on entering.*) How very unfortunate that you went to the city last night, you might have been instrumental in bringing the rascals to justice.

Mr. P. Rascals? What rascals? You speak in riddles, Miss Belmont. (*They sit.*)

Agnes. Haven't you heard?

Mr. P. Tell me to what you refer, and I will be able to answer more intelligently.

Agnes. Is it possible that no one has informed you how the house was broken into by burglars last night, how they dragged poor papa into the library and compelled him with threats of death to open the safe, how they got away with thousands of dollars and my beautiful diamond necklace, a present from a rich uncle in India—haven't heard a word of all this?

Mr. P. Not a word. You see, I fell in with an old acquaintance from California, and he insisted upon my staying with him in the city. Just my wretched misfortune. I am an expert with the pistol, and would like no better sport than to wing such game. Perhaps this is a relic of that performance. (*Showing a handkerchief.*) It hadn't occurred to me before, but I found this lying under the edge of the safe. Can this furnish a clue?

Agnes. Clue? Oh no, sir. That belongs to Dr. Fargo. Here in the corner are his initials "E. F.", Eugene Fargo, I placed them there myself.

Mr. P. Of course, if it belongs to him it is no clue at all. I thought it looked as if it had been used as a blindfold. One would hardly suspect him, however.

Agnes. (*Warmly.*) Suspect him! No, indeed. The bare thought of him in connection with such a crime is almost slander.

Mr. P. In his sober moments he would not attempt anything of the kind. But I am told that when fired with drink he is pretty reckless. The fact that he gambles a good deal might bring him in sore need, and make him desperate enough to do anything.

Agnes. (*Horrified.*) Fired with drink? Gambles? I don't think you know of what you speak. Dr. Fargo neither drinks nor gambles.

Mr. P. Not here, of course; but in different company he acts differently, so I am told. I suppose you know he is engaged to a young lady in the city. She is said to be quite a rattle-brain, and her influence over the doctor, I fear, is not the best. (*Agnes starts to her feet, then sinks into chair again.*)

Agnes. Sir, is this the truth you tell me? You must be in sport, sir. I cannot believe it.

Mr. P. My dear young friend, I have no wish to pain you, but I must insist that I am correct in my statements. It's no uncommon thing for a sober, quiet man to be engaged to a giddy-headed girl, and it surely is no uncommon thing for men to drink and gamble.

Agnes. I beg you say no more. Your words raise in my mind black clouds of doubt. They pierce me to the heart. I cannot believe, but there is some awful mistake. (*Weeps.*)

Mr. P. (*With a fiendish smile, aside.*) She is drinking the deadly hemlock of jealous suspicion. Sure death to love. (*Direct.*) Grieve no more over it, my dear Miss Belmont, but solace yourself with the thought that he is as good as the average of men. I'll not disturb you any longer. (*Drops letter on floor.*) Your noble nature revolts at such hypocrisy, and so does mine. But call up your powers of will and dispel every suspicion from your mind. (*Aside.*) S .e'll never take that advice. Ha, ha! I'll yet win her hand — and fortune. (*Exit R.*)

Enter COL. L. *and stops on seeing* AGNES *weeping.*

Col. (*Aside.*) Well, now, what's the occasion of all this moisture that rains from her beautiful eye, and washes the bloom from her cheek. I'll warrant there's a man at the bottom of it.

Agnes. (*Looking up.*) Is it you, Colonel? Oh! I'm the most wretched woman in the world.

Col. Your appearance testifies to that fact.

Agnes. Colonel, you're a friend, dare I trust you—

Col. A good many people have dared to trust me (*aside*) and afterward regretted it.

Agnes. Dare I trust you with a secret?

Col. Oh, ah, certainly.

Agnes. Mr. Patroni informs me that Dr. Fargo is—how can I tell you,—is very much addicted to wine drinking, and— he—goes with a rattle-brained girl in the city. (*Sobs.*) I want you to help me find out whether or not it is true.

Col. True? What does Mr. Burns, the poet, say? He says:
> Some books are lies from preface to finis,
> And some great lies were never penned.

That does not seem to pan out with me as it did with Burns, but it's true, anyway. That's one of the unpenned lies. It's such a whopper that nobody can find a pen large enough to hold it. Patroni would rather lie on sight than tell the truth on time without security.

Agnes. Oh, you don't know how much good it does me to hear you say so.

Col. You don't know how much good it does me to say so, either.

Agnes. Was there ever a man, Colonel, whom you owed—

Col. Hundreds of them.

Agnes. Whom you owed a debt of gratitude you never hope to pay? (Col. *nods.*) If not, you cannot know the joy your words inspire. I will believe him true until he is proven false. And yet, what object could Mr. Patroni have in thus accusing him?

Col. Here comes the sot himself, quiz him. I'll retire. (*Exit L.*)

Enter Dr. R.

Agnes. (*Joyfully.*) Oh, Gene, I'm so glad—(*checks herself, coldly.*) Good morning.

Dr. Good morning, darling. I couldn't come earlier, business in town detained me there all night.

Agnes. Pleasant business, no doubt.

Dr. Anything but that. Why do you think so?

Agnes. It's no matter, only I have been informed that you have a very agreeable patient whom you attend with great regularity.

Dr. I don't seem to get the drift of the joke.

Agnes. Joke! Of course it's a joke, a nice, agreeable joke. I did suppose there was one man who was perfectly honest and scorned hypocrisy, but my mind is changed.

Dr. Miss Belmont, will you have the kindness to explain yourself? (*Changing tone.*) Come, darling, you are nervous and hysterical from the excitement of the day. (*Takes handkerchief from pocket.*) I'll leave you for a time and go into the garden, perhaps Mr. Patroni is out there.

Agnes. If you see him, you'd better question him, perhaps he can clear up the mystery of my conduct.

Dr. I'll try, and see. (*Exit R.*)

Agnes. I cannot think him guilty, he doesn't act it. (*Sees letter on floor.*) What's this? (*Picks it up.*) Wonder if Gene dropped that when he took out his handkerchief just now. Addressed to Miss Jennie Goldenburg. I'll see whose it is, and return it to its owner. (*Opens.*) It looks like the Doctor's writing. (*Reads*):

DEAREST JENNIE:—It is possible that I cannot spend this evening in your delightful society, as I am invited to Belmont

Hill to drone the evening out in company with a tiresome person who persists in her efforts to thrust herself into my society. If I cannot find sufficient excuse for declining her invitation, I cannot see you for *two whole days.* To-morrow evening, darling, if not this. Yours at all times, E. F.

(*Tears letter into pieces and throws it on the floor.*) The perfidious wretch! The cool, diabolical hypocrite! Tiresome person indeed! *For two whole days!* How it must cause his tender heart to bleed. Papa and Cyril shall know how contemptibly he is acting. . (*Exit. R in a passion.*)

Enter COL. L, *with a newspaper. Sees pieces of letter on floor and picks them up.*

Col. Save the sweepings, is my motto.

Enter MISS P., *L.*

Miss P. What a noble husband you will make for some one, Colonel. You're so thoughtful, so saving of labor.

Col. (*Stuffing pieces in pocket.*) In short, quite a labor-saving machine. Had I got hold of those burglars, they would have taken me for a full-fledged threshing machine. When I was in the battle of the Boyne—

Enter Sx. *with a box.*

Su. Yhar's anudder lottery fortin, sah. Fred said de 'Spress man lef it arly dis mornin. (*Sets box on table.*) Ya, ya, ya! Suffin fine in dar, I reckon. Dey hab lots ob nice tings in de lotteries. I'm one ob 'em.

Col. (*Proudly.*) Unquestionably, unquestionably.

Miss P. (*Anxious to see it opened.*) Hadn't you better—ah, wouldn't it be well to open it at once, sir? It might be perishable. (COL. *turns front of box to her.*)

Col. Open it, please, open it. I'm in such a state of nervous trepidity that I cannot do it. (MISS P. *raises cover two or three inches and peeps in. Machinery inside blows flour into her face, eyes and hair Bus. of shaking flour off.*)

Su. Shure nuff, dar *was* suffin *fine* in dar. You's " de flower ob de family " now, Miss.

Miss P. (*Indignant.*) Lottery! I'll warrant Fred had a hand in that. (*Exits L, loftily.*)

Su. (*Aside.*) And some one else had a nose in it. (*Struts off, brushing off flour in imitation of* MISS P.

Enter MR. P., *R*; *looks for letter.* COL. *sinks into a seat and watches him over his paper.*

Mr. P. (*Aside.*) The letter is gone; by this time the leaven is well at work . (*Takes a seat.* COL. *steals up behind him, glances at his collar, nods, and seats himself again.*)

Enter DR., *R, with riding whip and hat.*

Dr. Here you are, Mr. Patroni. I have looked almost everywhere on the premises for you.

Mr. P. (*Aside.*) Now is my chance to insult the puppy. (*Direct.*) Well, sir, I hope you don't want to dose me. How *is* the pill business, now, doctor?

Dr. (*Surprised.*) Dose you? No; I only want to question you. Have you been saying anything to Miss Belmont derogatory to my character?

Mr. P. Suppose I have, what then?

Dr. Then, sir, you would prove it, or I would publish you as a liar. (COL. *peers nervously over newspaper.*)

Col. (*Aside.*) Correct.

Mr. P. Liar, sir! *You* call *me* a liar?

Dr. No sir; I simply said that if you have defamed my character you will prove it, or I'll prove you a liar.

Mr P. It's the same thing; I resent it. This difficulty can only be settled in accordance with the code.

Dr. Code! Bosh! This is too enlightened an age to talk of codes. Duelling days are done. None but brutes fight duels.

Col. (*Aside, over his paper.*) I'd rather be a brute than fight a duel.

Mr. P. None but cowards object to the code,—that's my opinion.

Dr. Your opinion is of vast importance; suppose I absolutely refuse to engage in any affair of honor with you?

Mr. P. In that case I would denounce you as a coward and a scoundrel.

Enter SN. *D in F; seizes* DR. *by the arm, and tries to drag him off.*

Sn. (*Excitedly.*) Doctah, doctah, dar's a woman down stair wot sent me up yhar in a hurry. Her chillen's all got de morphines, and she wants a bottle of measles to cure em. Has you got enny?

Dr. Wait a moment, Snowball. (*To Mr. P.*) Denounce me when and where you will. What you may say shall pass by me as the idle wind, for I utterly ignore both you and your barbarous code.

Mr. P. (*In a rage.*) Then you are a cowardly scoundrel!

Sn. (*Excited.*) Doesn't you resent dat, Doctah? Doesn't you resent dat?

Dr. (*Coolly.*) No, boy; I am above resenting a lie.

Sn. I ain't. De bible's agin lyin. (*Seizes whip from* DR.*'s hand, strikes* MR. P. *a sharp blow over the head with it, then falls back two or three steps.*)

Mr. P. (*Almost insane with rage.*) You black devil! That blow shall be your last. (*Draws dagger, and starts toward* SNOWBALL. COL. *dances around between* MR. P. *and* SN.; *draws his sword, and presents it nervously at* PATRONI's *breast.*)

Col. (*In a high key.*) Sir, if you have any kind of regard for your heart's blood, or your shirt front, desist from your sanguine purpose, or I—I I'll certainly inveigle you upon the point of my sword. But, perhaps you don't grasp my meaning?

Picture at close: Mr. P., *L of C;* Col., *R C;* Sn., *behind* Col. Dr.; *extreme R.*

CURTAIN.

ACT III.

SCENE I. *Interior of a doctor's office; small table at back, with lamp burning upon it; couch at R; chairs R and L; hook in scene at R; door in back and R.*

Immediately after curtain, groans heard without. Enter Sn. *D in F, doubled up with pain. Sees room is vacant and looks cheerful.*

Sn. Land ob goodness! Had dat fuss-fer-nuffin— Tonight dat doctah was yhar. Jes a wastin my sweetness on de desert air; now I'll rest my sweet self on a deserted chair. (*Drops into chair, crosses legs and sings.*): " Put my little shoes away"—in de pantry an leabe me in em. Clare to goodness I's stood round so long I's got a fearful rush of blood to de feet, but I reckon dar's room fer it. (*Takes out his watch, and thumps it twelve times on a chair.*) Time dat, doctah, war yhar. My chronometah has jes vibrated de hour ob twelve. Ef I warn't a fool, I'd tell dat doctah he's likely to hab an almighty sudden visitor to-night. Gorry, I'll tell; no, I won't nudder. Ef dat visitor didn't come, den Barney an me would git larfed at fer our susperspichun. Let him come, an I'll transcribe fer him, (*produces a large navy revolver,*) an my dose will be bout seben blue pills, to be well *shaken* before *taken,* ya, ya. Dat's a new-fangled bell punch, bound to attract attention when used. I'm one ob em. (*Hears step, hides revolver and feigns sickness.*)

Enter Dr. *D in F.*

Dr. Are you sick, Snowball? You look pale.

Sn. Not zackly sick, sah, dough I'm pale, as usual, but I's got a pain in my—in my somick, sah, an I wants jes a trifle ob medicine, suffin sweet, mixed wid a little rum to keep it from spoilin.

Dr. I guess you can keep it from spoiling. (*Steps off R.*)

Sn. I'll try ter git ar ter stay yhar all night. I'll sleep wif one eye open, or wif my mouf open, an dat will do jes as well. Ef dat chap comes— (*Taps place where revolver is concealed.*)

Re-enter Dr., *with a bottle and glass.*

Dr. Here is something that will give you immediate relief, I think. (*Pours medicine,* Sn. *drinks and dances wildly about, making faces.*)

Sn. Golemity, sah, ef dat's immejit relief, I doesn't choice eny.

Dr. Pshaw, that's nothing but a little capsicum and spirits.

Sn. (*Astonished.*) Cap,—which?

Dr. Cayenne pepper and spirits, that's all.

Sn. Dat's enuff. Tasted to me jes like de bizness ends ob foah quarts ob yeller jackets mixed up wif sulfiric asses. It doesn't zackly make de mouf water, ef it does de eyes.

Dr. Wring out your eyes, Snowball, and eat this apple to remove the taste from your mouth. (*Gives apple.*)

Sn. Tanks, sah; but dat's a mighty small apple to remove such a big taste from such a big mouf. (*Eats.*)

Enter BARNEY *D in F, holding his jaw; winks at* Sn.

Bar. Faith, an dochtor, I hev a foin pain in me tooth, ontirely Fwat does yez think, u'd better it?

Sn. Gib de gemman some ob dat immejit relief, dat balm of Gilead ye jest now gib me, and he'll tink he's a fine toof comb wif ebery toof achin fit ter break.

Dr. Has your tooth pained you for some time?

Bar. Some toime, is it? Shure an I've hed the tathe ache ivery day since I was born, sor.

Dr. If that's the case, you'd better have it extracted.

Bar. I don't know that, sor. Don't it *hort* a bit?

Dr. Oh, yes, *some,* of course; but it isn't long.

Bar. No, sor, not more than five or six fate long, anyhow. But it ud be me blackguard luck to hev the roots of them same tathe makin a double bow-knot clear undernath me toes. But fwat wud yez be afther chargin me, dochtor?

Dr. Our rates for extracting teeth are fifty cents for a single one or a dollar for three.

Bar. Well, I think I'll hev a dollar's worth pulled, thin. The others don't troable me onny, but it's a dale chaper accordin.

Dr. All right; I'll get the forceps and some cotton ready. (*Exit* Dr. *D in F.* Bar. *takes* Sn. *down L.*)

Bar. (*Rapidly, and in a low tone.*) Whist, now, an I'll tell yez. About dark I heard two men talkin under the bridge, an I listened says one, says he: be thayre promptly on toime, I hev a can uv powther ready, an we'll blow the nuisances into a thousand atoms. Ye'd little think who it wuz thet sed it. Be on yez guard now, by; I'll watch the road outside. Yez musn't slape a wink to-night, nagur. (*In usual tone.*) Wot's that dochtor afther?.

Sn. Pears to me he sed he'd git a coffin.

Bar. An does he pull tathe with a coffin? Faith, an I almost wish I wuz a dafe mute widout a tooth in me head.

Sn. You doesn't know what toof-ache is. Wait till your teef gits as big as mine. See dat toof dar on the off side? (*Shows it.*) Dat toof's achin now like sin, but I doesn't mine it.

Bar. Howly Moses! If I had a tooth loike that, I'd pull it with a string. (*Produces a string, and makes a loop in it.*) Thayre, hook that over yer bicupid, an the heft of the string will pull it. Thayre, now, sate yezsilf, an fasten the string to that hook. (Sn. *obeys.*) Now, throw yez head back gintly, an ye'll hev no more trouble wid yez tooth than a bank cashier hez wid his conscience. (Sn. *throws head back gently against string. Barney draws a revolver and thrusts it in his face.* Sn.*'s head flies back; he falls over the chair to floor, leaving tooth hanging to string.* BARNEY *holds up string and tooth and roars with laughter.*)

Bar. I think ye'll kape awake now widout trooble, an ef thar's any foitin to be done, ye'll feel in condition fer it. Jes tell the dochtor I've gone after the dollar. (*Exit* BAR. *D in F.* SN. *takes string from tooth and looks ruefully at both.*)

Sn. Golly, only one? I tougt the whole gang war comin out.

Enter DR. *with forceps.*

Dr. Where is that man with the tooth ache, and what was all that noise about?

Sn. I didn't yhar any, sah, I felt some noise, dough. (*Shows tooth to* Dr.) Dat's some ob Barney Moore's pickin. Dat's de wust job ob toof harvestin I's seen. (*Groans.*) Not de right toof at all.

Dr. (*Taking powder from phial on knife.*) Here is a powder that will make you feel more comfortable.

Sn. Is dat some more ob your Cap Sickum, sah?

Dr. No, this is all right. (Sn. *takes it.*) I'm glad that fellow is gone, for I want some sleep. It's nearly one o'clock, and I have a call to make at four. You take that blanket and make yourself as comfortable as possible, and I'll lie here on the couch. (Sn. *wraps himself in blanket and lies on floor down L.* DR *turns down lamp and sinks upon couch. Both are breathing heavily.*)

Enter PATRONI, *D in F, masked. Carries a three or four qt. can labeled gunpowder, and a revolver poised. Speaks low and distinctly.*

Mr. P. Aha, what isn't it worth to be born under a lucky star. I no sooner think of an explosion, than one of my worst enemies places a can of powder within my reach. (*Touches can with revolver.*) And now my star of fortune again favors me, by sending that black imp here, to meet the common fate with that white-livered hound. (*Points revolver at* DR.) What will not one do, prompted by desire for revenge, urged on by love—and fortune. (*Places can on stand with label to back, and places taper in nozzle.*) Blood I hate, it tattles; this tells no tales. If Clifford will only come to enjoy the ascension with them, I shall be happy. I hope Lafarge has made no mistake. (*Low whistle without;* MR. P. *listens. Whistle heard again.*) He comes, I hear the signal. (*Lights taper and hisses out*): Oh, how sweet is revenge! Sleep on now, fools, until to-morrow. For you it *is* to-morrow. The light of the only to-morrow you will ever know shines for you now. (*Points to taper.*) Farewell. (*Rubs his hands gleefully.*) I see the obstructions vanishing from my path. Farewell, a long, a loud farewell. (*Exit D in F. Enters soon after,* CYRIL.)

Cyril. All asleep? Must be some mistake. Could I have misunderstood the fellow? If it's a joke, it's a poor one to call a fellow up at this time of night. (*Sees taper.*) Queer lights they keep here. (*Examines can.* SN. *awakes, rises to sitting posture and immediately fires at* CYRIL.)

Cyril. Hold! Would you murder a friend? (SN. *fires again.* CYRIL *runs out D in F.* DR. *has sprung up bewildered, and rushes after him.*

Sn. Go it! I tink it's safer in de house. I'm fear'd ob gittin sun stroked, ef I go out sech an evenin as dis. Friends in a horn. I'm one ob— (*Revolver goes off as he holds it by his side. He caps into the air, then holds up his foot to examine it.*) By de holy mackerel, she am safe. I tougt that little foot had climbed de golden stair fer de las time. It's a miraculum she warn't tored all into little pieces no bigger dan a wash tub. (*Revolver goes off again.*) Dat 'volver's nerves am shattered. I am one ob em.

Enter CYRIL *D in F, hat over his eyes, followed by* DR. *with an ax.*

Dr. One attempt at resistance, villain, and I'll brain you. (SN. *is ready with revolver.* DR. *turns lamp up, and sees can on table; taper nearly burned down.*) Heavens! (*Blows out taper.*) What infernal plot is this?

Sn. Dat's wot he war fixin when I gub him one.

Dr. Gunpowder! (*Removes taper carefully, and pours powder into his hand.*) The can is filled with powder and ball. (CYRIL *is agitated.*) Wretch, what does this mean? (*Turns* CYRIL *to lights, peers into his face, falls back astonished.*) Clifford, Cyril Clifford, as I live. (*Sinks into a chair.* SN. *drops revolver; drops on his knees and groans.*)

Sn. Oh Lor, oh Lor, oh Lor!

Cyril. Yes, Cyril Clifford. Trapped by some scheming rascal, but innocent of any attempt to harm you.

Enter BARNEY *D in F, holding his head.*

Bar. Faith, an yez hev the spalpeen. (*Recognizes* CYRIL.) Ah, and is it yez, me young gintleman, caught in sich a scrape. It's Barney Moore that wud be glad to see yez safe out uv it. But I recognized yez under the bridge, and I suspected yez.

Cyril. Suspected me, sir?

Bar. I'd a been glad to let yez go, but me conscience sez to me, sez it: ef he's mean enough to try it, he's mean enough to get caught at it.

Cyril. Beware how you accuse an innocent man. I was under the bridge to get a man to do some blasting for me in uncle's park. Of this (*pointing to can*) I know nothing, except that I was sum--

moned here to see a sick friend; by whom summoned I do not know. I found the door unlocked, and entered; saw the can, and light; and while looking at them, Snowball tried to shoot me.

Sn. Oh, fergib me, massa Cyril; I didn't know it wuz you, deed I didn't.

Bar. Didn't I see yez wid that same can only yisterday?

Cyril. (*Looking at can.*) Yes, I bought that can yesterday to do the blasting, and left it in an outer cellar; how it came here, I know not.

Sn. I believe you, sah; I believe you.

Bar. One more question—

Sn. You'd bettah let your questions stop your yawp. Why wasn't you yhar to join in de fracas?

Bar. Thot's it. I hadn't more than left here, whin some one gintly let a pile-driver drap on me head, an I fell as stiff as the Cardiff Giant. The first thing me hand grasped, on comin to, wuz this knife. (*Shows one.*) I reckon the chap wot give me the tap, is the one thot drapped it. Hev yez sane it before?

Cyril. The knife is mine, but I cannot explain it. Everything is against me, but I am innocent.

Dr. This is indeed a suspicious showing. I can scarcely believe you guilty; (Col's *face at window.*) but circumstantial evidence is against you. Many a man, Mr. Clifford, has suffered death on less conclusive evidence.

Cyril. I admit it; and our quarrel, or rather, my insolence, at the time of our last meeting, only gives the matter an uglier look. Do with me as you like; I am resigned and innocent. (Col.'s *face disappears from window.*)

Dr. I will take no legal action at present, but will give you an opportunity to find the real culprit, if you can. It will also give you an opportunity to go abroad, if you are guilty.

Cyril. I see you suspect me, doctor, but I will never confirm your suspicions by running away. When you want me, you can easily find me.

Dr. I confess I cannot quite strangle my suspicions, but I owe you no ill will.

Cyril. I'll prove my innocence, or die in the attempt. (*Exit.*)

Dr. (*To* Bar. *and* Sn.) Don't mention this occurrence. Time will show where the guilt lies. We'll have the experts out. Remember, success depends upon silence. (*Exit D in R.*)

Bar. Did he have the can when he camed in?

Sn. (*Very low-spirited.*) I dunno.

Bar. An did yez go to slape afther losin thot tooth?

Sn. De doctah gub me suffin wot made me sleep. When I waked up, he war stan'n jes whar you iz. Den I takes de resolver so, an — (*Showing him. Revolver goes off, pointed at* Bar.)

Bar. (*Seizing a chair.*) Ye grimy divil, wad yez be afther killin me, too?

Sn. No, sah, no, sah. I didn't mean to hab it go off. (Bar.

32 A SOLDIER OF FORTUNE.

puts down chair.) Dat 'volver's as uncertain as a mule. Shoot de
'volver. (*Throws it out the window. It goes off outside.*) Jes heah
dat, now.

Bar. Ef ye'll let the blarsted thing alone, it'll shoot itself yit.
But let's lave here, we've had fun enough. Ef the by is innocent,
we must find it out. Divil take the dirthy dodge that did the dade.
(*Exit both D in F.*)

CHANGE.

SCENE II. *Scene same as Act I.*

Enter MISS P. *R, with a novel.*

Miss P. I wonder where that bundle of aggravation, known as
Fred, is keeping himself. If he isn't here at study hours, I'm not
accountable. (*Sits R of table, facing it, and reads.*)

Enter FRED *cautiously, R, with a large placard labeled in large
letters: "To please me, Squeeze me," and fastens it on* MISS P.'s *back
at shoulders; slips off, and comes in D in F, whistling loudly.*

Miss P. Take your grammar, Fred, and study your lesson.
I'll hear yesterday's lesson soon. (*Continues reading.*) FRED
spreads Grammar on table; takes a pin from his coat.)

Fred. (*Aside.*) I'll put up a pin where it will give some one the
grand bounce. *Fixes pin in chair up; takes large cigar from pocket,
puts it in mouth; sits with feet upon center-table; takes out a pack of
cards, and is looking at them when*

MR. B. *enters L, 1 E, and peers over* FRED'S *shoulder.* MR. B.
gives him a sharp slap.

Fred. You hold a good hand, Governor; dont want me to follow suit, I suppose?

Mr. B. Follow suit, eh? (*Gives him another slap.*) I'm the one
to follow suit. Is this the way you employ your study hours?

Fred. (*Whining.*) Pity if a feller can't look at some little chro-
mos what he gits at Sunday-school, without gittin slapped all to
pieces for it. (MR. B. *seizes cards and cigar, and throws them off.*)

Miss P. Give me the grammar, Freddie, I'll hear yesterday's
lesson. (FRED *obeys.* MR. B. *sits and listens.*)

Miss P. What is a verb, Freddie?

Fred. (*Sullenly.*) Verb is the name of anything. (MISS P.
shakes her head.)

Miss P. What is an adverb?

Fred. I dunno.

Miss P. What is a participle?

Fred. Word derived from the office of—I dunno.

Mr. B. Do you know anything about nouns, Fred? (*Fred
nods.*) Decline "table."

Fred. I might do that, but you don't catch me declining dinner.

Mr. B. Why, Prucilla, the boy knows no more of grammar than a thug does of theology.

Fred. (*Brightening up.*) Try me on adjectives, Govey. I know all about them things.

Miss P. (*Aside to* FRED.) Those things you mean, Fred.

Fred. If you call me mean Fred, I'll steal your false teeth and give 'em to the Colonel.

Mr. B. That will do. Come, compare the adjective, good.

Fred. Trot one out, and I'll compare it as good as I know how.

Mr. B. I want you to give the comparison of that particular adjective, good.

Fred. Now I twig. Good, better, best; wet, wetter, west; soon, sooner, sudden; pork, beef, mutton; cuss, custard, cust; boil, boiler, bust. There! I guess the gilt edged thing to do next is to parse, so I'll parse out doors. (*Sidles up D in F.*) Miss Peterson, don't forget to conjugate the verb, love, for the Col. I heard you at it yesterday. (*Imitating.*) I love, you love, he's lovely. (*Exit D in F.*)

Mr. B. (*Angry.*) That's a sample of what novel-reading, humane society meetings and Foreign Missionary Associations, will do. That boy's conduct is the disgraceful result of a disgraceful course of training, Miss Peterson.

Miss P. Of course. I am responsible for the whole of it.

Mr. B. (*Walking floor.*) You have undertaken to teach that boy, and you imposed the task upon yourself. Now you spend your time worrying over the poor, dear animals, instead of giving that boy a little of your time and attention.

Miss P. Well, I can't see that my neglect of him is any worse than your own. You had the training of him nine years before I ever saw him. But of course, I am solely to blame for his wretched behavior. (*Exits R, indignant.*)

Mr. B. Perhaps there is some truth in what she says, after all. The almighty dollar has had too much of my attention, and the boy too little; I fear we are both to blame. If the present storm blows over, and I ever am again on my legs, that worthless boy shall know more of a father's care and attention. (*Enter SN. with letter, hands it and exits.* MR. B. *opens, and reads.*)

MR. BELMONT,

Dear Sir:—It pains me to inform you that your title to the estate you now occupy, is invalid. By a technicality you were defrauded in the purchase of the estate, which fact has been made clear to me by the attorney of the claimant to the property. The name of the rightful heir is not known to me, neither will said attorney divulge it at present. Come down prepared for a compromise. Yours, J. P. SMITH, Attorney-at-Law.

(MR. B. *sinks back in chair.*) Beggar! There is no hope, or Smith would never write in that strain. This is a gambler's, a stock gambler's fate. (*Groans, and staggers off R.*)

Enter AGNES *and* MR. P., *L.*

Mr. P. I have just been reading, for the twentieth time, that old story of Pyramus and Thisbe. What nobleness of spirit to sacrifice everything, even life, for love.

Agnes. The story doesn't affect me that way, at all. I think them a couple of fools.

Mr. P. Please don't say so, Miss Belmont. Think how poor Pyramus must have felt when he supposed his love was torn to pieces by a lion.

Agnes. That's no worse than to be torn to pieces by many another thing, gunpowder, for instance.

Mr. P. (*Starts slightly alarmed. Aside.*) Can she suspect?

Agnes. I suppose you have heard it rumored that an attempt was made to assassinate the doctor, the other night. It seems some one went there after the doctor, and from the outside got an inkling of the matter.

Mr. P. Yes, I heard of the rumor. I came near being killed in that same manner, myself. I was traveling in Italy. My guide drugged and robbed me, and then attempted to explode a keg of powder under my bed.

Agnes. Nothing but a fiend incarnate would think of such a deed. I hope there is a hereafter, and a serious one, for such vile wretches. But I was not aware before, that you had traveled in Europe.

Mr. P. Ah, but haven't I? You should visit the Coliseum by moonlight, glide through the streets of Venice, or gaze upon the glorious crest of the Jungfrau, towering heavenward in all its grand and spotless purity.

Agnes. (*Earnestly.*) The dream of my life has been to visit those places, of which I have heard so much.

Mr. P. (*Seizing her hand passionately.*) Agnes, dear Agnes, that dream may prove a bright reality. A single word will open the way. Only say you will be mine, that you will flee with me to distant lands, and you shall spend a lifetime, if you will, among those charming—

Fred. (*Without, calling loudly.*) Aggie, I say, Agnes, where are you? (*Enter* FRED *with a bottle of hair oil.* MR. P. *drops* AGNES' *hand.*) Whose hair oil is this?

Agnes. It's Miss Peterson's. I'll take it to her.

Fred. No, you don't. She'll get it by paying for it.

Agnes. I'll tell her you have found it, then. Excuse me for a few moments, Mr. Patroni. (*Exits R.*)

Mr. P. (*Aside.*) Curse that young cur's interference.

Fred. (*Aside.*) Wonder what Goose Grease is grumbling about now. (*Exit* MR. P. *D in F.* FRED *inspects the chair where he has left the pin.*) Still ready for business. (*Sets bottle on stand.*) Miss Peterson won't advance any stamps on this hair oil, I know. It's too thin, anyhow; it must be thickened. (*Steps off R; brings on a bottle of mucilage.; holds it up.*) Mucilage, that's the huckleberry. About 'alf and 'alf will make her laugh. (*Pours mucilage into hair oil.*) There! That would be a better joke if the young thing didn't wear store hair. It won't hurt, but it will hold. (*Exit R, with mucilage, leaving hair oil.*)

Enter Sn.; *walks very slowly and lazily.*

Sn. Golly! I's dat tired and weak I couldn't pull a settin' bumble bee off it's nest. (*Drops into chair where pin is. Bounds into the air.*) Oh! how my conscience do prick me. (*Takes pin off chair.*) Shoot de pin back. Some of Fred's crookedness. Dat's an eberlishun of childish innocence dat orter stan' in close nearness to a club. (*Sees bottle on table; takes it up and reads label.*) Potation ob Bay Rum. Potation? Dat means good ter drink; rum is; I'll try it. (*Drinks, and makes a face. Reads.*) Fer de har. I'll try it. Hope it's bettah for de har den it is fer de taste. (*Rubs it into his hair.*)

Enter Fred, R.

Fred. Hello! What you up to, Blackball?
Sn. Limberin my locks wif dis potation.
Fred. Pomatum, you numskull. A potation is something to drink.
Sn. Dat's my logic, else I shouldn't ob drunk enny ob it.
Fred. Jerusalem! Have you been drinking that stuff?
Sn. Sartin I hez. Wh–wh–what am it?
Fred. *(Horrified.*) You'll be as stiff as a poker in less than ten minutes. It has mucilage in it.
Sn. (*In agony.*) Muckleage? You doan mean it. You're tryin to cod me.
Fred. That dose will cod you soon enough, if you don't do something.
Sn. Oh Freddy, my deah boy, fer de love ob hardenin' humanity tell me what to do to keep me soft.
Fred. (*Tearing leaves out of grammar.*) Here, swallow this, and the paper will absorb the mucilage. Then run to the doctor, and let him pump you. (*Exit Sn., D in F, chewing paper.*) Ha, ha! Perhaps he will quit tasting of everything, after this. Strange that I should happen to tear that everlasting review out of my grammar for Snowball to digest. (*Looks off L.*) Hello! Here comes the Colonel; hasn't been here for three days. I'll keep watch of him. It might be he has drawn another grand lottery prize. (*Crawls behind couch.*)

Enter Col. L.

Col. (*Peering about at room and furniture.*) Yesterday, a penurious beggar; to day, a second Crocus. Strange that fortune's wheel, with one swift turn, should whirl me into possession of these massive walls and specious grounds. Fortune's wheel, accept thanks. Heir to this vast property! I can scarcely believe my

eye-glasses. Nothing repulsive about it, anyhow. I am free to
wed, ha, ha! This estate will sell for at least two and five
aughts. On that I can get an interest of six. That will give
twelve and three aughts. That's enough for Prucilla and Alphonso. They must not know yet the name of the heir apparent,—no, no,
I don't mean that, of course. *This* heir is not a parent. Name of
the heir to the property a secret! Ha, ha! Good! Soldier of
Fortune, I should say so. Perhaps I don't grasp my own meaning.

Enter Mr. P., *R, and* Cyril, *L.* Fred *crawls out, and exits un-
noticed.*

Mr. P. (*Bowing low to* Col., *then to* Cyril.) Good morrow,
my lords. In all humbleness I bear, to each of you, a message
from the master of Belmont Hill.

Ida *enters up L, walks across, and stops before going off.*

Col. We are fortunate in being able to hear the master's pleasure.
Cyril. Out with it.
Mr. P. I deliver my message, not by express command, but
on account of frequent hints thrown out to me. To you, most
noble sword-bearer, I convey the implied wish of Mr. Belmont
that you seek for quarters elsewhere.
Col. (*Aside.*) Wants to excommunicate me from my own
house, eh? I don't believe it. (*Direct.*) Am I to understand
that my room is better than my regiment—I should say, better
than my company?
Mr. P. That some would take it so, is true, most valiant wear-
er of the blue. (*To* Cyril.) And to you, my lord of the tin can,
your venerable uncle sends greeting, and says you will be welcome
here *after* you have accounted for that little episode of recent midnight occurrence.
Cyril. (*Very angry.*) Allow me to remark, sir, that uncle
never told you anything of the kind, nor has he ever hinted it;
and any one who asserts such a thing for a fact, is the most out-
rageous liar in the universe.
Mr. P. Do you mean to insinuate that I lie?
Cyril. Insinuate nothing. Insinuation I'll leave for coward
rogues. I say that if you claim Mr. Belmont sent you here on
such an errand, you lie. Now make the most of it.
Mr. P. (*Coolly.*) Humph! Coward rogues sounds immensely
well in the mouth of a midnight assassin.
Cyril. Do you so far forget yourself as to insinuate that I am a
midnight assassin?
Mr. P. Oh, no. I insinuate nothing. I call you so, and so I
will call you when chance permits us to meet. Brave lad, to seek
to take a rival's life by stealth, because too chicken-hearted to meet
him fairly. You're a promising youth, you are.

Cyril. (*Aside.*) I'll die rather than be thus goaded. (*Direct.*) Sir, you shall answer for this in your own chosen way. I'll send a friend to make arrangements.

Mr. P. 'Tis well, 'tis very well. I'll give you practice with powder and ball outside of a tin can, I hope. (*Exits L, laughing.* IDA *exits R U E.*)

Cyril. (*In a rage.*) Curse his villain heart! What mischief is brewing and all for him? He slanders the Doctor, until Agnes refuses to see him; he tries to rule the house, and uncle with it; he insults you and me on every occasion. Would that he, vile wolf, had never entered here to mar the happiness of this peaceful fold.

Col. (*Looking knowing.*) My dear young friend, you have named but a small portion of his wolfish depredations. But I must seek my lady love and beat my light catarrh. (*Exit R 1 E.* CYRIL *sinks into a chair.*)

Enter IDA, *L U E; comes quickly down and drops on knees at side of* CYRIL'S *chair. Bus. of his noticing her.*

Ida. Oh, sir, did you ever have occasion to ask a favor of one you esteemed highly, but from whom you feared a refusal?

Cyril. (*Smiling.*) I cannot recollect of having been so situated.

Ida. I am so situated at present, Mr. Clifford, and I want your advice.

Cyril. My advice is, go plead your own cause. If the one you speak of has a soul, nothing can foil the argument of your sweet voice and glistening eye.

Ida. The one of whom I speak has a soul, for thou art he.

Cyril. I? You surely cannot plead in vain. If anything in my power to grant, your request should not remain unspoken.

Ida. Thank you, sir; your kindness is unbounded. And yet, the cause I would plead is your own, as well as mine.

Cyril. Please name it.

Ida. You have just now, while momentary anger held sway, challenged *him* to mortal combat. Only a few days ago, you vowed that you loved me. I would that for one moment I might revive that love so you would pledge your word that you will withdraw the challenge at once. Say, oh say that you will grant my request, and make me happy. It surely is within your power; say you will.

Cyril. To grant your request, dear madam, is not within my power. My honor has been most basely assailed, and before it even my will cowers in abject servitude. Therefore, much as it pains me to do so, I must refuse.

Ida. Do not say that. I beg this poor boon more for your sake than mine. Listen to reason. You have challenged *him.* *He* has the choice of weapons, and the choice will be pistols, with which his skill is almost superhuman. Many a time have I seen him cut short a glowing wick, at twenty paces; I never saw him

fail. How easy would it be for him to cut short a human existence.
I will not leave you until you promise. Even were you to slay
him, the canker of remorse would gnaw away your happiness with
the thought that you had been the messenger of death to one of
your fellow men. I beg of you, let me not plead in vain. (CYRIL
paces the floor in great agitation.)

Cyril. (*Stopping before her.*) Miss Lovewell, perhaps you little
know how this struggle pains me, but I must be firm. As you
not long since said to me, so say I now to you. Honor, honor
must remain inviolate.

Enter MR. P., L.

Mr. P. Madam, this way.
Ida. Sir, I will not.
Mr. P. Will not? Remember the old father, and the prospect
of his intimacy with the grate.
Ida. (*In terror.*) I'm coming, sir. (*Aside to Cyril.*) Refuse
to keep the engagement, while there is yet time. If you love me,
do. (*Exits submissively to L, with* PATRONI.)
Cyril. (*Amazed.*) Intimacy with the great. What strangely
potent spell those words cast about her! It's beyond my shallow
comprehension. (*Exits R 1 E.*)

Enter COL. *and* MISS P., *R. U. E.*

Col. (*Speaking as they enter.*) It was perfectly sublime, perfectly
glorious, perfectly—I might say, very nice indeed. It reminded me
of a scene that occurred in the battle of Chicken Hominy, the
day after I met a beautiful auburn blonde, and fell head over
heels in—
Miss P. In love, sir?
Col. No, no; fell head over heels into a rifle pit, just as I was
about to help the beautiful auburn blonde to dismount.
Miss P. And you weren't indulging in tender love glances, at all?
Col. Oh, certainly not at all, only at the beautiful blonde,— I
would say, only at the beautiful blue Danube. But, speaking of love,
so to speak, reminds me that my stay in Mr. Belmont's residence is
short; and before I depart, it would please me to make you some
trifling gift.
Miss P. Not stay longer with Mr. Belmont?
Col. No, dear madam, no. On leaving, what could I give you
as a token of slight esteem—I mean, as a slight token of esteem; a
memento to remind you of the many happy days we have passed
here?
Miss P. Anything that would serve as a reminder of you,
would be prized most highly. (*Gives him a tender glance, then
turns partly from him in confusion.* COL. *sees placard, and hastily
steps to her side, and encircles her waist with right arm; makes no
effort to release herself.*) Why, what do you mean, sir, by taking
such premature liberties?

Col. I only squeeze you in order to please you.

Miss P. Oh, my, for shame, sir! Such undignified language. Let me go. Who said it would please me? (COL. *releases her, and takes off placard, and shows it to her.*)

Col. My information was derived from this poetic announcement.

Miss P. (*Shrieks.*) Oh, horror! That wretched Fred. (*Sinks into chair ; COL. sits by her side. They partially face audience.*)

Enter FRED, *D in F, with a fish pole, which he cautiously hooks into* COL.*'s wig.*

Col. About that trifling present. Now, suppose I were to say myself; (MISS P. *catches her breath;*) that would surely be trifling. Would it be quite satisfactory to you?

Miss P. Oh, you have taken me so by surprise, Colonel—I should say Alphonso Adolphus;—so unexpected, I hardly know what to say. It wouldn't be just exactly polite for me to refuse, would it? No young lady wants to be considered impolite—so—I'll—say—yes. (FRED *suddenly swings wig into air on pole, showing* COL'S *bald head.* COL. *and* MISS P. *spring to their feet.* MISS P. *stands amazed.* COL. *dances about the room in the wildest excitement, with his hands spread over his shiny crown.*)

Fred. (*Loudly.*) Two souls with but a single thought,
Both know the Colonel's hair is bought.

CURTAIN.

ACT IV.

SCENE I. *Grounds surrounding the Belmont residence. Beautiful vegetation. (Might be interior of mansion, in hall or parlor.) Two or three rustic seats.*

Enter CYRIL, *R.*

Cyril. (*Looking at watch.*) Twenty minutes past seven. The hour is fixed at ten. That this is the last time I shall see the glorious sun leap from her burnished portals in the east, the last time my senses will take in the charming freshness of a summer morn, is more than probable. Oh, what a fool was I to let that underhanded, scheming villain spring this trap upon me. Why did I let him goad me into challenging him, the very thing above all else he desired. With Fargo and myself out of his path, he hopes to win the hand of Agnes. (*Enter* COL. *U R. To* COL.) Are the arrangements all completed?

Col. They are complete.

Cyril. Colonel, if I die—

Col. Tut, tut; never say die, until you are dead. 'Tis a word of ill omen. Methinks it hath a sickly sound.

Cyril. If I fall to-day, Colonel, I want you to do all in your power to reconcile Agnes and the doctor. She surely will not marry this fellow if he succeeds in this day's venture. I am almost certain he has used some trick to alienate their affections. (*Col. bows.*) I have made my will. Agnes inherits my property if she marries the doctor, not otherwise. Poor girl, she will need it, for her father is on the verge of bankruptcy.

Col. Bankruptcy? You surprise me. I supposed him worth millions.

Cyril. Plainly, Colonel, he has almost nothing. He was wealthy, but he suddenly struck a bad run in stocks, and now he can scarcely say he has a roof to shelter him, for I understand the title to Belmont Hill is anything but good. About the sum total of his worldly goods is comprised in a lot of old certificates of railroad stock, probably almost valueless. He has been unable to settle with me within many thousands of dollars. Poor man, I pity him. But I must go and bid them all farewell. Uncle and Agnes think I am about to start on a long journey, and perhaps I am. Be at the place of meeting promptly.

Col. Delay at such a time cannot be considered dangerous.

Cyril. Delay at such a time is weakness. (*Exit.* FRED *steals in and listens.*)

Col. Can it be true that Mr. Belmont is almost a beggar? Now what am I, the heir, to do? Belmont has always enjoyed luxury. Fitznoodle has always enjoyed poverty. Isn't it best to have a change made? For Fitznoodle the doors of Belmont's house have ever stood ajar. Must Fitznoodle go to that kind old man and say: Sir, you have shown me many favors, but as I am heir to this estate, you must step out and down? Something struggles within me. What it is, I know not. Perhaps it is gratitude, perhaps it is an accumulation of wind on the stomach. Be it what it may, I am resolved. The rightful heir must be conjured back, unknown, to the realm of shade whence he came. He must kindly collapse and leave this pleasant home undisturbed, save by the footprints of the hand of Providence. Time steals away, and so must I. Farewell, sweet dreams of home. Farewell, Prucilla dear. A beggar now I roam, and I—I— go to help fight a duel. (*Exit.*)

CHANGE.

SCENE II. *A wood. A lone tree up stage at R, prepared for lightning. Hudson river at no great distance.*

Enter CYRIL, *followed by* BARNEY *and* SNOWBALL. SNOWBALL

carries a case of pistols which he places on ground up C. CYRIL
walks back and forth up stage. Sn. *and* BAR. *come down.*

Sn. Land ob goodness! Dis am de wust job I's eber been
called upon to honah wif my presence. I hab a good will to keery
dat pore boy away bodily.

Bar. Ye'd bethter let the lad alone. Ye'd git hort. He's dead
certain to fight, and he's certain dead if he does fight. Leastways
that's what he thinks.

Sn. Pears to me we might run de udder set off de track.

Bar. Yez can't switch em off so aisy. The only chance is thet
the blackguard gintleman will consint to draw cuts for first shot.

Enter DR. *R* 1 *E.*

Dr. Does the boy still persevere in his foolishness?

Bar. Thot he does, sor. An it's a good name ye have called it,
sor. But honor sticks hard in the poor by's crop.

Sn. Dat ar honah am suffin I's not quainted wif, an I loan
want no interductions to it nuddder.

Bar. A foin sojer ye'd be widout honor.

Sn. Sojer? No sojerin fer me, sah. I doesn't choose any. I
am one ob em.

Dr. Wouldn't you be a soldier to save your country, Snowball?

Sn. No, sah. What 'ud country be good fer to me, ef I wuz
dead? Nuffin. Nuffin's good fer nuffin when you's dead, sah.

Bar. By, ye're a coward.

Sn. Hope I is. I'd rudder lib ten yeahs a coward den be dead
twenty yeahs a hero. (DR. *goes up to* CYRIL.)

Dr. Can nothing dissuade you from your purpose? I hope you
do not really consider this an affair of honor. (*Distant thunder.*)

Cyril. (*Not unkindly.*) Doctor, could pleading have influenced
me, I had yielded long ere this; but words can no more turn me
from my course than can the gentle rains of summer revive the
fallen leaves cut off by last year's biting frosts. The die is cast.
A fortune teller looked into my hand when I was but a boy, and
perhaps her words were prophetic. She said, "I can see nothing
there but the number twenty-three, and that is dimmed by blood."
Doctor, I am twenty-three to-day. (*Looks off R.*) But here they
come.

Enter MR. P., *accompanied by a friend.*

Dr. Is there no way, Mr. Patroni, by which this difficulty can
be amicably settled?

Mr. P. There is none, sir. (*Enter* COL., *L.*)

Cyril. Let us not parley. (*To* PATRONI.) You are an expert
with the pistol, I am not. I have this proposal to make. We will
cast lots to see who shall shoot first. That will give me some
slight chance. Come, sir, is not that fair?

Mr. P. Verdant as ever, I see. Do you not know that is a

matter for our seconds to settle? But I'll accept the condition. I hope you have now no excuse for refusing to keep this engagement. (*Thunder at distance.* COL. *puts two slips of paper numbered 1 and 2 into a hat.* PATRONI *goes down R.*)

Col. (*To* P.'s *second.*) Select one of these pieces of paper. If you get number one, your friend is to have the first shot. Otherwise, Mr. Clifford's ordnance will be first heard from.

Mr. P. (*Aside, while they are drawing.*) I trust my lucky star still shines. But if I get number two, I draw and shoot the fellow without formality, and trust to luck in escaping.

Bus. of drawing. Much excitement. MR. P.'s *second draws No. 1.* DR. *shades eyes with his hand.* SN. *drops on his knees and weeps.* BAR. *draws sleeve across his eyes.*

Mr. P. (*Fiendishly.*) Ha, ha, ha! Fool! (*Goes up R.* CYRIL *comes down L.* MR. P. *moves case of pistols to R, with his foot. Lightning and thunder.*)

Cyril. (*Sadly, but firmly.*) I see the result in your faces. 'Tis yours to stay, 'tis mine to go. This only hastens by a few years the inevitable. (*Shakes hands with friends. They show deep emotion.*)

Sn. (*Rising suddenly, and speaking firmly.*) Look a y har, frens. I wants ter tole yer suffin. Onst dar war a young nigger, and dat young nigger got de small-pox, bad. An wunst dar war a young white man, an dat young white man took keer ob dat young nigger all de while he war sick. Stuck right by him at de risk ob his own life till he got well; (*lightning and thunder;*) keered fer him like a mudder. Got him eberyting heart could wish; an sat by his bed nights when no udder would come anigh. All because dat young white man's heart war full ob sympaty wif de sufferin an de afflicted. I doan know ef dat young man's name is on enny ob de church account books, but I reckon dar's a right smart chance standin to his credit in de big book de angel keeps up dar. (*Points heavenward.*) Dat pore nigger is before you. Dat noble young man stans dar. (*Pointing to* CYRIL.) Oh, Cyril, boy, I's no hero. I's only a coward, a pore, miserable, cowardly nigger. But to-day I'll gib up dat life you sabed, dat life which belongs to you. (*Goes up and drops on his knees before* MR. P. *who is leaning against the lone tree.*) Oh, sah, lem me stan up dar in place ob dat deah boy, to be shot down. Lem me be his substitute, an de angels will whisper sweet words to you in yer dreams, and make yer happy. (*Frequent flashes of lightning and heavy thunder.*)

Cyril. Snowball, desist, I beg you. I appreciate your motives, and I thank you more than words can tell, but you cannot take my place. Live, and be happy.

Mr. P. Yes, leave me, nigger, or I'll shoot you with as little compunction as I would a dog.

Sn. Do it, sah, do it. Only let dat deah boy lib. (MR. P. *kicks* SN., *who falls over backward, and then crawls away. Brilliant lightning and heavy thunder.*)

Mr. P. Come, hurry up. The storm will soon be here, and we will be drenched with the rain.

Col. May I have the privilege of interpolating a few words before this ball opens?

Mr. P. I care not, so your words be short ones.

Col. There are some reasons why this duel should be indefinitely postponed.

Mr. P. Now valiant, what next?

Col. The chief reason is that Mr. Clifford has not been insulted, as no man of honor can possibly be insulted by a felonious felon.

Mr. P. Hold! Do you know what you are saying?

Col. I think I do. This fellow Patroni, *alias* Proudfit, *alias* Thomas, Richard and Henry, is a bigamist. He claims to be the husband of Ida Lovewell; while he has another wife now looking for him.

Cyril. (*Staggering backward into* DR.'s *arms.*) He Ida's husband? Oh, how blind I have been. (*Thunder and lightning.*)

Mr. P. (*Standing erect, with arms folded.*) Anything else?

Col. Oh, yes. This is the man who drags old gentlemen out of bed at four o'clock in the morning, and compels them to unlock their own safes.

Mr. P. Go on, spy. (*Aside.*) And then die.

Col. This is the man who sneaks into offices with cans of villainous saltpeter to destroy the lives of somniferous persons there somnifering. This is the man who writes love letters, and signs other people's names to them, and leaves them where they will destroy the peace of a happy, innocent pair. (DR. *much agitated. Continues to* CYRIL, *looking off R.*) This is the man who thinks he can insult a gentleman, and yonder comes an officer to arrest him.

Mr. P. If you have exhausted your store of information, vile wretch, die!

Quick as a flash, draws revolver from his pocket and snaps it at COL. *who smiles blandly.* MR. P. *looks at revolver, throws it aside, snatches one from case near him.* COL. *draws sword, about to rush upon him. He shoots* COL., *who clasps his hand over his breast, but does not fall.* MR. P. *then levels revolver at* CYRIL, *and is about to fire, when a flash of lightning, amid an awful crash of thunder, descends the tree, striking* MR. P., *who falls dead at foot of tree. All much stunned.* DR. *does not see that* COL. *is shot, but runs to* PATRONI *and makes a rapid examination.**

Dr. (*Rising slowly.*) No need of an officer. He who directs the thunderbolt has summoned him before a higher than earthly tribunal. He is dead. (PATRONI's *friend goes up and kneels over his body.*)

* The flash of lightning may be produced by firing a loose hempen string, well soaked in spirits of turpentine. Drop the string from above and at the same moment fire a gun to assist the sheet iron in producing thunder. Where it is impossible to produce this scene on the stage it may, by a slight change of wording, be represented as occurring outside.

Col. Cyril, my boy, our work is done. It is growing dark. It's—time—to—go—home. (*His sword falls from his hand. He gasps, staggers backward and falls into SNOWBALL's arms. SN. sinks upon his knee and supports him. Others gather around and form picture.*)

CURTAIN.

ACT V.

SCENE. *Same as Act I. Mirror hung up at back. Several months after last scene.*

MR. B. *discovered reading a newspaper. Enter* AGNES, *R U E.*

Agnes. I'm so glad, papa, this long expected day has at last arrived. Won't it be splendid to have the Colonel here again? I declare, I look upon him as quite a hero.

Mr. B. How about his attendant, the Doctor; of course it won't be splendid to have him here again.

Agnes. Now, papa, just think what bad taste I would display were I to say right out I'm glad the doctor is coming.

Mr. B. Such a thing is not to be thought of, I suppose.

Agnes. Oh, yes indeed, it's to be thought of, but not spoken of. But I'm suffering terribly from curiosity to know how the Colonel managed to discover that man's trickery. You know the Doctor wouldn't allow the subject to be mentioned to him before they started South, as he feared the excitement would bring on an attack of hemorrhage.

Enter CYRIL *and* IDA, *R.*

Mr. B. I hope we will find the dear, silly old fellow entirely recovered. Had it not been for him, you, impetuous youth, would have come sadly off from that day's difficulties.

Cyril. Indeed you are right, uncle. It could not have been other than a sad day for me.

Ida. How thankful should I be that it was as it was. How little happiness would have— (*Stops confused.*)

Cyril. Before you say more, let me explain to uncle. Uncle, you know I am going away for a few months, and although you may think it premature, I have asked Miss Lovewell, whom I confess, I love well, to become my wife when I return. I was to consult you before I made my choice, but you see we got to talking over matters matrimonial, and really it was all settled before I knew it. I hope you are as pleased with my choice as I—I should say as Agnes is.

Mr. B. Another clear case of impetuosity. But I confess you could not have made a better selection, even with assistance in choosing. Well, children, accept the old man's blessing. I have at last come to the decision that though matches may not be made in heaven, but few happy ones are made up from bank accounts. I am thankful that in my darkest hour I did not use my misfortune as an inducement for Agnes to marry where I was foolish enough to wish to have her.

Ida. I'm glad you didn't, uncle. Filial duty may, perhaps, demand the sacrifice of life, but a sordid, unholy marriage, never.

Mr. B. You have never told us how you came to be the victim of that person's duplicity.

Ida. There is little to tell. Father was in cramped circumstances. That person supposed him wealthy, while he supposed that person wealthy. I became the victim of the misunderstanding. Our marriage was kept secret, I think, for fear of retribution, while my tongue was tied with threats of exposure of father's pretended guilt.

Mr. B. The subject is a painful one, let us drop it forever. (*Enter* FRED *D in F.*) What need to harbor sullen thoughts
That make us neither wise nor good?
Let us think of more agreeable things.

Fred. (*Coming down.*) I'll tell you some more agreeable things. I want you to buy me a span of little twin white mules, both of them exactly alike.

Mr. B. A mule is a dangerous plaything, my boy.

Fred. Buy me a bycicle, then.

Mr. B. Worse and worse.

Fred. Buy me,— (*thoughtfully*,) buy me a tooth brush, then. (*Braying of a mule without.*) What's that? Seems to me I hear a sweet small voice. (*Runs up, looks out of window, then comes down.*) Snowball, with a span of little white beauties with ears as long as yard sticks. Whatever made you do it?

Mr. B. Snowball told me you wanted them, and so I thought to surprise you.

Fred. You're a darling daddy, a real broth of a boy. I'll be good more than an hour to pay for that, see if I don't. (*Gives his father a hug and kiss, and runs off D in F.*)

Mr. B. (*Much pleased.*) A very impulsive boy. Warm-hearted and impulsive.

Enter Sn. D in F.

Sn. De duet am yhar, sah. Didn't ye yhar em wabble, sah? Dey's a beautiful milk-white pair, sah. I'm one ob em.

Cyril. Be careful, Snowball, that you don't let any of us *see you* wabble.

Sn. Tally one fer you, sah. Dat stroke ob wit makes me transpire at ebery pore.

Cyril. Say perspire, not transpire. (*Laughing.*) You make a break down stairs, and don't let me see you up here again for an hour. (Sn. *exits hastily D in F, then sticks head back in at door.*)

Sn. Did you say an hour, Massa Cyril?

Cyril. Yes, I said an hour. (Sn. *dodges out, but immediately sticks head in again.*)

Sn. A houah! Dat must be a heap ob time. It's more than my repeater eber 'repeats. Don't yer forgit it. I'm one ob em. (*Exit.*)

Mr. B. Snowball, like some other members of the household, is almost insane with delight because the Colonel and the Doctor are coming.

Cyril. I'm glad to see him so happy. I have never given him an angry word since he pleaded to be my substitute. He shall not want for anything while I have the power to prevent it. If he outlives me he shall be remembered.

Sn. (*Sticking head in at the door.*) Dey's comin, ladies an gemmen. Come right out into de conversatory, an you can see em easier den a full man can see a full moon. (*Exit all D in F.*)

Enter FRED *L U E. Face dirty, and clothes covered with dust.*

Fred. May I be kicked again if ever I attempt again to curry a mule's heel with a case knife. (*Sees image in glass.*) Hi, you young sardine, come out here and let me hit you once, and to-morrow they'll be carrying you off to the soap factory.

Enter SN. *D in F.*

Sn. Ef yer doesn't hold yer yawp, dey'll be keerryin *you* off to de soap factory fore yisterday, you great mud-turtle you. You *wouldn't* make bad soap, dough, kase you's all lie and grease. You's jes like a ribber, yer mouf's bigger dan your head. (*Holds his watch to his ear.*)

Fred. I say, hash preserver, can you hear the vibrations of that remarkable piece of mechanism?

Sn. It ain't got em yet. It's neber had nuffin cept de measles an de mumps, an de hoopin cough.

Fred. What makes you so stupid? You talk as if a watch were a person.

Sn. Ef a watch am not a person, it is a'most, fer it has face, an hans and upinion, an hair in de spring; (*opening it at his side, so audience can see it has no works.*) an sometimes it's only a good er nuffin hard case at dat. But I only took it out to git de key, so I can gib you a grand selection from de grand opera ob Sing Sing. (*Introduces song.* FRED *joins. Invisible chorus, if convenient.*)

At close of song enter D in F MR. B. *and* COL., DR. *and* AGNES.

Mr. B. You don't know how it pleases me to see you looking so well, Colonel.

Col. Oh, I always look well, except for a few weeks after I have been shot, and then I always look badly especially if I have been shot through the lungs. There's something very disagreeable about being shot through the lungs, for a fact.

Agnes. (*Clinging to* DR.'s *arm.*) I suppose there is nothing now to prevent the Colonel from telling us all about his adventures here last summer?

Dr. Nothing. He is at liberty to tell his story with any amount of variations.

Col. Since I quit telling my reminiscences of army life, I have seemed to grow unskilled in the art. I hope you will pardon any seeming veracity that may manifest itself.

Agnes. I was so delighted to recover my beautiful diamond necklace. How did you find out who robbed the safe?

Col. Oh, that was as easy as telling a lie. I made a beautiful piece of spatter-work of the two early worms. Had some indubitable ink on a sponge, and spotted them. The day after I discovered some of it on our paste-diamond gent's neck. Soon as they were treed, it was an easy matter to club them down, you know. Perhaps you don't grasp my meaning?

Mr. B. Yes we do. How about the seance at the Doctor's?

Col. That was perfectly simple work, for a simpleton. I dogged his steps and dodged his presence. That night I was a little too late. I glided up as he waltzed out, and thinking he had relinquished, I followed him to the abode of his confederate. When I again reached the office, our colored friend's artillery was so noisy within, that I didn't choose to enter for fear I would disturb him, and get shot through the lungs.

Sn. (*Coming down, and producing revolver.*) Yhar it am, sah. Loud one, ain't it?

Col. (*In terror, clasping his hands over his breast.*) D-d-don't bring it here. That's the one he shot me with. Go bury the beastly thing a thousand fathoms beneath the ground.

Sn. (*Putting it away.*) But it ain't loaded, sah.

Col. Of course it isn't. But that doesn't prevent them from going off. (SN. *goes up.*)

Mr. B. How did it happen the Californian's revolver did not go off when he first fired to shoot you? Perhaps it was providential.

Col. Yes, sir. All owing to Providence and precaution. I employed a professional to extract it from his pocket, extract the loads, and return it again to its place.

Agnes. But the letter, Colonel, the letter?

Col. Like Snowball's revolver, it can speak for itself. (*Produces letter composed of pieces pasted on a whole piece.*) I saved the pieces, that's all. 'Twas a good imitation of the Doctor's chiropody, but not quite good enough.

Enter CYRIL, IDA *and* MISS P.

Col. (*Skipping up to* MISS P., *and shaking hands.*) Oh, dear madam, your presence here creates a palpitation here. (*Puts hand on his breast.*) A sight of you awakes the most exchanting memories; stirs up the thoughts of yore, and brings to mind sweet scenes of summer days, of babbling brooks, of flowers green and red—

Fred. And flour fine and white.

Mr. B. Freddie, be quiet.

Col. (*Good-naturedly.*) Yes, of flour fine and fair, and fish poles in the hair. But those happy days are gone, I fear, forever. I have something to say, and our friends may as well hear it. To you I pledged my troth. In my mind, there is no change; no, nor elsewhere about me. That's the difficulty. When I asked you to be mine, I was indeed a Soldier of Fortune, for vast wealth stared me cheerfully in the face. Now I am a poor soldier of misfortune, whom to wed were worse than not to wed at all.

Miss P. Don't say that, dear. I have no wish to marry wealth. Name and fame are more to my taste.

Col. Of name I surely have a plenty.

Fred. (*Coming down.*) Look here, folks, our Colonel is getting too proud. I've got a rig on him that will give his pride a tumble.

Mr. B. Fred, if you don't keep quiet, I shall be compelled to remove you from the room.

Fred. (*Drawing the* COL.*'s sword from the scabbard.*) Remove nothing. I'll hack the first feller that touches me; so you may as well hear me out. You know, Govey, when you were so near dead-broke, last summer? Expected to lose this shanty, and were just saved by those old worthless stocks taking a turn up, and by the feller that owned this place failing to turn up—remember that, don't you, daddy?

Mr. B. I don't understand how you—

Fred. How I happened to know, eh? I'm up to snuff, of best quality. As Snowball says, I'm one of em. Well, you don't know the feller to whom this rightfully belonged, do you? (MR. B. *shakes his head.*) That's where I have the advantage.

Col. (*Aside to* FRED.) Do be quiet, Fred. Not another word.

Fred. (*Paying no attention.*) The chap didn't die, at all. He gave the property up to you because, he thought, to keep it would inconvenience the family. (COL. *slips off R.*)

Mr. B. What nonsense! The gentleman relinquished his right to the estate with the understanding that his name was to remain secret three years. He shortly afterward died.

Fred. Pooh! He isn't dead, I tell you. (*Sees* COL. *is gone. Darts off R.*)

Cyril. What can the boy mean? Some of his jokes, I'm thinking.

Ida. He seems very much in earnest.

Re-enter FRED, *holding the* COL.*'s arm.*

Fred. (*To* COL.) If you hadn't come, I would have told it worse than it is. Ladies and gentlemen, here is the rightful heir to Belmont Hill.

Mr. B. Can it be possible? You the heir who relinquished the estate of his own free will?

Fred. That's the kind of a fellow he is. (*Aside.*) I always thought him a little queer. (*Direct.*) I overheard him when talking to himself about giving it up. (*All gather around to shake hands.* MR. B. *quietly exits to R.*)

Cyril. You're one of the true nobility, sir.

Agnes. You have our everlasting gratitude. You saved us from financial ruin, and raised us again to wealth and happiness.

Dr. If generosity is its own reward, you must be enjoying an enviable recompense.

Ida. The deed is better than name, or fame or fortune. It shows the noble promptings of a noble heart.

Fred. To sum it all up, you're the hero of the day, The Soldier of a Fleeting Fortûne, but the Boss Brick of the Universe. In short, you do yourself proud. I surrender to you my sword. (*Hands* COL.'S *sword to him.*)

Enter MR. B. R, *who whispers to* SN., *who exits R.*

Mr. B. (*Coming forward, and taking* COL.'S *hand.*) My dear friend, I hardly know how to find words to express my gratitude for the sacrifice you made for us in the day of our misfortune.

Col. Don't try to find them, sir. The fewer you find, the better. Actions speak louder than words. Your actions show your pleasure, and that for me is a superabundance of sufficiency.

Enter SN. R, *bearing a box.*

Su. Yhar's a box fer de Cunnel, marked "Gran Prize ob de Lancaster Lottery."

Col. (*Nervously.*) Remove it, please. Transfer it to some other portion of the house. I was not aware that I possessed a ticket in that, or any other grand gift enterprise.

Cyril. You'd better open it here, Colonel. If it's a joke, let us all enjoy it.

COL. *cautiously opens the box, takes out a piece of paper, glances at it, trembles, and hands the paper to* CYRIL *to read.*

Cyril. (*Reads.*) National Bank of Commerce, pay to the order of Alphonso Adolphus Fitznoodle, two hundred thousand dollars. B. G. Belmont.

COL. *goes over and grasps* MR. B.'S *hand, and attempts to speak.*

Mr. B. Not a word. It's yours by right. It is chiefly through your generosity that I am again in condition to have a check of that amount honored.

Col. (*Going to* MISS P. *and taking her hand.*) This is a most glorious outcome of a previous most meager income. I think you and I can subsist on the revenue from two and five aughts, so we'll set the day, and then away to lovers' fields elysian.

Su. (*Coming down to* COL.) Goin into de matter-o'munnial lottery, is you. (*Produces a paper from his pocket, unrolling it.*) Reckon you'll want suffin ter put de little gran prizes into. (*Dis-*

plays the baby's stockings.) Ya, ya, I'm one ob em. (*Passes stockings to* Col.)

Col. (*Giving them to* Miss P. Keep them, keep them, as a gift from a Soldier of Noble Fortune.

Cyril. You're a soldier of several fortunes. Miss Peterson has a handsome property in her own right. She has kept the fact secret, for fear some man would want to marry her for her fortune.

Col. I am dumbfounded; I am surprised.

Agnes. Time has shown the truth of a remark I once made, that beneath a vain and frivolous exterior ofttimes lies a soul more noble than that of belted knight or lofty-titled squire.

Dr. The experiences of the past year are instructive. Let us all to-day make new resolves that shall carry us above the sordid aims of life, and inspire within us a love for the noble, the good and the true.

Ida. Our experiences confirm the fact that noble deeds, rather than fluent words, influence most our lives and happiness. (*All come down.*)

Mr. B. I want to hear from our kind Soldier of Fortune on the relative power of words and deeds.

Col. (*Stepping forward.*) Words are sky-rockets. They go fizzing, and banging about, making a brilliant display and doing some little service. Deeds are cannon balls. They go straight to their destination, annihilating, pulverizing and deoderizing every· thing that insinuates itself into their parabola. I hope you grasp my meaning.

POSITIONS:

Mr. B.	Fred.	Snowball.
R, Dr. and Agnes.	Col. and Miss P.	Cyril and Ida, L.

CURTAIN.

9 783337 306922